Misquotes in *Misquoting Jesus*

Why You Can Still Believe

Dillon Burroughs

NIMBLE BOOKS LLC

Nimble Books LLC

ISBN: 0-9777424-6-6

Copyright 2006 Dillon Burroughs

Cover image: Albrecht Durer's *The Crucifixion* via
http://www.cts.edu/ImageLibrary/Public_domain.cfm

Last saved **2006-06-09.**

Nimble Books LLC
2006 Medford Suite C127
Ann Arbor, MI 48104-4963
http://www.nimblebooks.com

Contents

Publisher's Comments

I am proud to publish this book because of its worthy message: that when you hear confusing messages in confusing times, you can and should still believe.

AMAZON UPGRADE

If you bought this book through Amazon.com, you can purchase Amazon Upgrade for a nominal fee.

RIGHTS

U.S. and international republication rights are available on request. Please send e-mail to rights@nimblebooks.com.

ABOUT NIMBLE BOOKS

Our trusty Merriam-Webster Collegiate Dictionary defines "nimble" as follows:

```
1: quick and light in motion: AGILE  *nimble fingers*

2 a: marked by quick, alert, clever conception,
comprehension, or resourcefulness  *a nimble mind*  b:
RESPONSIVE, SENSITIVE  *a nimble listener*
```

And traces the etymology to the 14th Century:

```
Middle English nimel, from Old English numol holding
much, from niman to take; akin to Old High German neman to
take, Greek nemein to distribute, manage, nomos pasture,
nomos usage, custom, law
```

The etymology is reminiscent of the old Biblical adage, "to whom much is given, much is expected" (Luke 12:48). Nimble Books seeks to honor that Christian principle by combining the spirit of *nimbleness* with the Biblical concept of *abundance:* we deliver what you need to know about a subject in a quick, resourceful, and sensitive manner.

Author's comments

For most students of the NT, a book on textual criticism is a real yawn. The tedious details are not the stuff of a bestseller. But since its publication on November 1, 2005 *Misquoting Jesus* has been circling high near the Amazon peaks. And since Bart Ehrman, one of North America's leading textual critics, appeared on two of National Public Radio's programs (the Diane Rehm Show and Fresh Air with Terry Gross)—both within the space of one week—it has been in the top fifty sellers at Amazon. Within three months, more than 100,000 copies were sold. When Neely Tucker's interview of Ehrman in The Washington Post appeared on March 5 of this year the sales of Ehrman's book shot up still higher. Mr. Tucker spoke of Ehrman as a "fundamentalist scholar who peered so hard into the origins of Christianity that he lost his faith altogether." Nine days later, Ehrman was the guest celebrity on Jon Stewart's *The Daily Show*. Stewart said that seeing the Bible as something that was deliberately corrupted by orthodox scribes made the Bible "more interesting…almost more godly in some respects."…Within 48 hours, *Misquoting Jesus* was perched on top of Amazon."[1]

November 1, 2005 marked the start of a revolution in the way postmodern readers view the text of the Bible. With the release of Dr. Bart Ehrman's *Misquoting Jesus*, the everyday reader of religion has been allowed access into the often mysterious field of New Testament textual criticism, opening eyes and providing more questions than answers regarding the compilation of the sacred Christian scriptures.

Publishers Weekly's starred review boldly proclaims on the back cover of *Misquoting Jesus*:

> "Engaging and fascinating…[Ehrman's] absorbing story, fresh and lively prose, and seasoned insights into the challenges of recreating the texts of the New Testament ensure that readers might never read the Gospels or Paul's letters the same way again."

At the time of this writing, *Misquoting Jesus* continues to stand at the number one spot in hardcover religion sales. A paperback edition and foreign language translations are also in the works. Over 250,000 copies of the hardcover edition have sold in the first four months of the book's publication, with no slowdown in sight. These alarming trends, along with the overwhelming amount of media

---

[1] Daniel B. Wallace, "The Gospel According to Bart." Accessed at http://www.bible.org/page.asp?page_id=4000.

response for the title, have not escaped the notice of the conservative, Evangelical Christian community.

Reactions have varied greatly. Many preachers and devout Bible fans have labeled *Misquoting Jesus* (and even Bart Ehrman) heresy, simply dismissing it without a fair read. On the other end of the spectrum, there are the numerous scholars and Christian leaders who have embraced the popularity of *Misquoting Jesus*, proclaiming it an accurate portrayal of church history and the New Testament's transmission. However, a growing number of individuals (including myself) have chosen to believe that there is a third option. While *Misquoting Jesus* may include some accurate information about portions of the New Testament's history, many aspects are skewed to make the author's point, and stands on very flimsy historical evidence.

Granted, regardless of one's position on *Misquoting Jesus*, there will be controversy. However, *Misquotes in Misquoting Jesus* desires to highlight what Ehrman does get right, while pointing out several places where he crosses the line from facts to fiction and explanation to exaggeration. In the end, we will see that despite Ehrman's outstanding academic credentials, major claims of his *Misquoting Jesus* are not only inaccurate, but deceiving to the everyday reader.

Of course, I do not claim this book will be perfect, either. I admit up-front my bias as an individual who still holds to the traditional teachings of Christianity, including supernatural events such as the virgin birth of Jesus and the resurrection of Christ. Yet despite my bias, I am open for discussion with those of you who have sincere objections or questions based on what you will read in this book. Please feel free to dialogue with me via my personal email at dillonburroughs@hotmail.com. I would be glad to hear your thoughts on *Misquotes in Misquoting Jesus* and share together in this journey of learning.

Author biography

As a speaker, writer, and advocate for the Christian faith, Dillon Burroughs has appeared in numerous locations nationwide and abroad. On subjects related to Christianity and culture, Dillon's speaking or written works have appeared on James Dobson's *Focus On The Family*, *The New York Times*, *The Washington Post*, (SRN) Salem Radio Network news, Moody Radio Network, iLife Network, Leadership Journal, NBC affiliates, and many other media outlets.

Dillon's work, *The Da Vinci Code Controversy* (Moody Publishers), was featured at the 2006 National Moody Pastor's Conference in addition to receiving media exposure in both mainstream and Christian sources nationwide, including an initial printing of over 20,000 copies, a rare achievement for a debut author.

In addition, Dillon has written or edited works with several of today's top Christian personalities, including Dr. Tony Evans (President, The Urban Alternative), Dr. John Ankerberg (Host, *The John Ankerberg Show*), Dr. Michael Easley (President, Moody Bible Institute), and Dr. Gary Chapman (author of the NY Times bestseller *The Five Love Languages*). His upcoming works include *Get in the Game, The Spirit of Truth and Error: World Religions,* and *The Spirit of Truth and Error: New Religious Movements.*

Dillon Burroughs is a ThM graduate from Dallas Theological Seminary in addition to graduating with a B.S. degree in Communications from Indiana State University. He lives in the Indianapolis, Indiana area with his wife, Deborah, and children, Ben and Natalie.

Acknowledgements

I would like to personally thank those thinkers and scholars whose writings and research have greatly enhanced the making of this book. These include Dr. Daniel Wallace, Dr. Darrell Bock, Dr. Craig Blomberg, Dr. John Ankerberg, and Dr. Michael Easley.

Certainly, Dr. Bart Ehrman is deserving of my deepest gratitude. Though he is of a different persuasion on many theological issues, his intellect challenges me to greater dedication in my studies. His impact remains enormous in the field of New Testament studies. I look up to many of his accomplishments and only pray we shared more values on spiritual matters. I hope my work only represents well-intended differences regarding his arguments and that he understands my heart for him is not arising from anger, but out of honor and respect.

My deepest thanks to Mark Tobey, a good friend, brother, and former editor of Moody Publishing. He has been the one person most influential in encouraging my early publishing. A warm thanks also on this project to my new friends at Nimble Books. True to their name, they have produced and responded more quickly than even most magazine editors I have encountered. All I can say is, "Wow! Keep up the great work!"

A special thanks to my best friend and wife, Deborah, for listening to my ideas, putting up with my early mornings of writing at Starbucks, and for standing beside me through every moment of the process. I love you! To my kids, Ben and Natalie, I love you so much! Thanks for making Daddy's life so special!

Lastly, my thanks to Jesus Christ, the one who fuels my faith and writing. May he be honored through these words.

NIMBLE BOOKS LLC

Chapter 1: *Misquoting Jesus* in the Media: NPR to Comedy Central

> "Sometimes Christian apologists say there are only three
> options to who Jesus was: a liar, a lunatic or the Lord," he
> tells a packed auditorium here at the University of North
> Carolina, where he chairs the department of religious
> studies. "But there could be a fourth option—legend."[2]

The *Washington Post's* Neely Tucker recently overheard this statement while sitting in on Dr. Ehrman's religious studies class at the University of North Carolina. For a professor who has helped edit the Greek New Testament and writes frequently in the area of New Testament Studies, this quote strikes me as rather far fetched. However, as the article later states:

> There are dozens of other examples in "Misquoting
> Jesus," things that go to the heart of the faith, things
> that have puzzled scholars for centuries. What actually
> happened to Jesus of Nazareth, there on the sands of Judea?
> Was he a small-time Jewish revolutionary or the Son of God?
> Both? Neither?
>
> These ancient questions have been the guideposts to
> Ehrman's life. His take on them -- first as devout believer
> in biblical inerrancy, then as a skeptic who rejects it all
> -- suggests a demand for black and white in an arena where
> others see faith, mystery and the far traces of the
> unknowable.

This only represents the foundation of the media's fascination with *Misquoting Jesus.* Ehrman has recently been mentioned on CNN, NPR, the Discovery Channel, A&E, National Geographic, The History Channel, *The Diane Rehm Show,* and even Comedy Central's *The Daily Show* with Jon Stewart. The news buzz has certainly helped, impacting both offline and online culture where *Misquoting Jesus* made the about.com list of "Books that will change the way you look at Christianity."[3]

---

[2] Neely Tucker, "The Book of Bart: In the Bestseller 'Misquoting Jesus,' Agnostic Author Bart Ehrman Picks Apart the Gospels That Made a Disbeliever Out of Him," *Washington Post*, March 5, 2006. Accessed at http://www.washingtonpost.com/wp-dyn/content/article/2006/03/04/AR2006030401369.html.
[3] http://altreligion.about.com/od/jesusmysteries/tp/xtian.htm

Of his nineteen books, *Misquoting Jesus* has become his first bestseller. He has, as one review mentioned, learned how to take something *really* complicated and make a sound bite out of it.

This has been especially true with the world's recent fascination with *The Da Vinci Code* book and film. As an expert source regarding its impact, Ehrman said he "likens the phenomenon to the excitement in the 19th century when deluded masses thought Jesus would return in 1844. The novel's impact on religious ideas in popular culture, he says, is 'quite unlike anything we've experienced in our lifetimes.'"[4]

Even Ehrman's local newspaper, the *Charlotte Observer*, has noted Ehrman's outstanding position as a scholar on the New Testament text and as bestselling author. Commenting on his thoughts regarding alterations in the Bible's transmission, he notes, "When I talk about the hundreds and thousands of differences, it's true that a lot are insignificant. But it's also true that a lot are highly significant for interpreting the Bible."[5]

In the same interview, when asked, "If we don't have the original texts of the New Testament—or even copies of the copies of the copies of the originals—what do we have?" Ehrman responded, "We have copies that were made hundreds of years later—in most cases, many hundreds of years later. And these copies are all different from one another."[6]

This style of scholarship combined with popular sentiment has fueled a number of his interviews. For instance, on *The Diane Rehm Show* featured on National Public Radio, December 8, 2005, Ehrman said, "There are more differences in our manuscripts than there are words in the NT." While the statistic might be true, his implications are that the differences point out problems in finding a core text for the New Testament, a much larger and more important issue.

Why the popularity on a book regarding New Testament textual criticism? The field, studied only by a small percentage of scholars, now stands on the front book racks at Barnes and Noble and Borders. Dr. Daniel Wallace, professor of New Testament at Dallas Theological Seminary and executive director of the

[4] http://www.cnn.com/2006/SHOWBIZ/Movies/05/01/decoding.davinci.ap/index.html
[5] Ehrman in an interview with Jeri Krentz, *Charlotte Observer*, December 17, 2005 [accessed at http://www.charlotte.com/mld/observer/living/religion/13428511.htm]
[6] *Ibid.*

Center for New Testament Textual Studies, provides his observations on the book's blockbuster success.

First, Jesus sells:

> Why all the hoopla? Well, for one thing, Jesus sells. But not the Jesus of the Bible. The Jesus that sells is the one that is palatable to postmodern man. And with a book entitled *Misquoting Jesus: The Story Behind Who Changed the Bible and Why*, a ready audience was created via the hope that there would be fresh evidence that the biblical Jesus is a figment.[7]

Second, it appeals to skeptics:

> More importantly, this book sells because it appeals to the skeptic who wants reasons not to believe, who considers the Bible a book of myths. It's one thing to say that the stories in the Bible are legend; it's quite another to say that many of them were added centuries later. Although Ehrman does not quite say this, he leaves the impression that the original form of the NT was rather different from what the manuscripts now read.[8]

Third, it represents the first major book on the issue for the popular audience in recent years:

> According to Ehrman, this is the first book written on NT textual criticism—a discipline that has been around for nearly 300 years—for a lay audience. Apparently he does not count the several books written by KJV Only advocates, or the books that interact with them. It seems that Ehrman means that his is the first book on the general discipline of NT textual criticism written by a bona fide textual critic for a lay readership. This is most likely true.[9]

In the end, it seems that multiple factors converge in the marketing and success of Ehrman's latest book. However, the critical concern for Bible-believing readers lies in the accuracy of the actual information, along with the masses reading and agreeing with views that are inconsistent with the facts of the Church's history. For those arguing for an accurate transmission of Scripture, and especially of the New Testament, a response to the evidence in *Misquoting Jesus* is a critical need. This is true both for the scholar and the pastor in this case, as Ehrman's work has leapt from the classroom to the coffeehouse as the latest read for the educated individual.

---

[7] Daniel B. Wallace, "The Gospel According to Bart." Accessed at http://www.bible.org/page.asp?page_id=4000.

[8] *Ibid.*

[9] *Ibid.*

Chapter 2: What *Misquoting Jesus* Gets Right

Dr. Craig Blomberg of Denver Seminary provided one of the first academic reviews on *Misquoting Jesus* from a conservative perspective. In his work featured in the *Denver Journal*, he writes:

> Thus a substantial majority of this book provides information already well-known and well-accessible in other sources, such as Bruce Metzger's works on the text and transmission of the New Testament (including one that Ehrman himself recently helped to revise), but in a slightly more popular form that is likely to reach a wider audience.[10]

Scholar Ben Witherington agrees. "Bart Ehrman is both an interesting person and an engaging lecturer. He speaks well, he writes well, he obviously has a gift for what he does. I like Bart though I find his spiritual pilgrimage troubling…"[11] The consensus among conservative Evangelical writers tends to paint a picture of the book as a general overview charged with slight sensationalism and a rocky personal background.

Even those with the most negative of reviews have commented on the quality of parts of Ehrman's work. For instance, J.P. Holding writes, "To be fair, the bulk of this book is unobjectionable history without any scent of controversy. As such it has value as 'Textual Criticism 101' but it has numerous quite serious problems interspersed with the neutral narrative."[12]

Yet despite the view of conservative writers, Bart's knowledge in the field is extensive. An author of nineteen books, Ehrman has personally studied with Dr. Bruce Metzger at Princeton Seminary, considered *the* authority on New Testament textual criticism in North America. His professional memberships reveal the status only few scholars obtain, including the Studiorum Novi Testamenti Societas, Society of Biblical Literature, North American Patristics Society, Institute for the Arts and Humanities, and the Academy of Distinguished Teaching Scholars. When Ehrman draws conclusions outside the

[10] http://www.denverseminary.edu/dj/articles2006/0200/0206.php
[11] http://benwitherington.blogspot.com/2006/03/misanalyzing-text-criticism-bart.html
[12] http://www.tektonics.org/books/ehrqurvw.html

traditional boundaries of church history, therefore, he does so very intentionally, keenly aware of the differing views.

Just *how* intentional these differences are can be hard to determine. As a contribution to textual criticism, Dr. Wallace notes:

> *Misquoting Jesus* for the most part is simply NT textual criticism 101. There are seven chapters with an introduction and conclusion. Most of the book (chs. 1-4) is basically a popular introduction to the field, and a very good one at that. It introduces readers to the fascinating world of scribal activity, the process of canonization, and printed texts of the Greek NT. It discusses the basic method of reasoned eclecticism. All through these four chapters, various snippets—variant readings, quotations from Fathers, debates between Protestants and Catholics—are discussed, acquainting the reader with some of the challenges of the arcane field of textual criticism.[13]

While Wallace provides challenging arguments against portions of the later chapters, he provides a general approval for the major summaries given in the early parts of the book. The structure of Ehrman's books makes it even more "strategic" in this sense, since readers will find themselves over halfway through the book before the major controversial issues are presented.

Blomberg provides a similar summary:

> Most of *Misquoting Jesus* is actually a very readable, accurate distillation of many of the most important facts about the nature and history of textual criticism, presented in a lively and interesting narrative that will keep scholarly and lay interest alike… Successive chapters treat, in brief, (1) the formation of the Hebrew and Christian canons, (2) the mechanics of copying a text in the ancient world and in the early transmission of the Christian Scriptures, (3) highlights in the history of the production of increasingly critical editions of a reconstructed Greek New Testament, along with the kinds of changes, both accidental and intentional, that scribes introduced into the thousands of manuscripts still in our possession, thus necessitating those reconstructions, (4) key post-Reformation textual critics involved with the production of the most well-known reconstructions, from Simon to Westcott and Hort, (5) modern methods of textual criticism, combining external and internal evidence, with several of the more interesting examples of significant changes in the New Testament, (6) more tantalizing examples of theologically motivated changes, and (7) similar examples where the social world of the scribes led them to introduce changes in the meanings of their exemplars. A brief conclusion returns to

---

[13] Wallace article.

his personal story, reiterating how, in light of the
numerous changes that preclude us from saying we either have
the original texts or can perfectly reconstruct them, he
finds it impossible to hold to biblical inerrancy or
inspiration (or even less strict forms of evangelical
Christian faith) and insinuates (without ever saying so in
so many worlds) that reasonable persons should come to
similar conclusions.[14]

So, what, exactly does *Misquoting Jesus* get right? In summary of the above comments and an observation of the book's text itself, Ehrman's book *does* provide much of the historical information regarding the history of the New Testament's transmission in an accessible way everyday readers can easily understand.

Specifically, Ehrman's book traces many of the major markers in the New Testament's transmission:

- The early compilation of the New Testament books.
- Transmission during the pre-Nicean church (pre-A.D. 325).
- Copyist's habits during the medieval period.
- The reconstruction of the Greek New Testament by Erasmus and others at the time of the printing press.
- Early texts discovered in the 1800-1900s and their importance in Bible translations today.
- The transition from the Byzantine text-type to an eclectic Greek text incorporating the best available manuscripts.
- The importance of textual criticism for Bible readers today.

In these areas, his efforts are to be applauded. Not only has he unearthed much of textual criticism's history for a popular audience, he has once again highlighted the importance of the New Testament text at a mainstream level.

Even in his hotly disputed chapters (chapters 5-7), his introduction to Chapter Five "Originals That Matter" provides an important discussion regarding the distinction between the number of manuscripts that agree on a verse's reading versus the early age and quality of a particular reading. While his illustrations may not all add up in the end, his modern English examples

---

[14] http://www.denverseminary.edu/dj/articles2006/0200/0206.php

provide readers a smile and even laughter, as he challenges readers to compare some of the differences in the Greek text that was written in a running script rather than like our English language.

His example of *isawabundanceonthetable* still cracks a chuckle whether one agrees with the book's premise or not (Is it really *I saw abundance on the table* or something else?) As a scholar providing information for a popular audience, Ehrman definitely delivers. But, as we will soon see, there is a big difference between making difficult information accessible and making certain it is accurate.

Chapter 3: Will the Real New Testament Please Stand Up?

The central controversy in Ehrman's *Misquoting Jesus* is that since we do not have the originals of the New Testament writings or even copies of the originals, then the New Testament we have today cannot be original and certainly not the inspired Word of God. He begs the question, "Can the real (original) New Testament text be discovered?"

In order to prove his line of reasoning, Ehrman distorts several points of debate from a one-time historical issue into a pattern that must somehow necessarily be the norm in throughout other New Testament books. As one review notes:

> What most distinguishes the work are the spins Ehrman puts on some of the data at numerous junctures and his propensity for focusing on the most drastic of all the changes in the history of the text, leaving the uninitiated likely to think there are numerous additional examples of various phenomena he discusses when there are not. Thus his first extended examples of textual problems in the New Testament are the woman caught in adultery and the longer ending of Mark. After demonstrating how neither of these is likely to be part of the originals of either Gospel, Ehrman concedes that "most of the changes are not of this magnitude" (p. 69). But this sounds as if there are at least a few others that are of similar size, when in fact there are no other textual variants anywhere that are even one-fourth as long as these thirteen- and twelve-verse additions.[15]

Misquoting Jesus has a tendency to create controversies where they do not exist. In doing so, he pushes for his readers to share in his frenzy of a book riddled with errors. Specifically, he argues that the "very words" (p. 5) of the original text have been misplaced. However, determining the original among variant reading is not the impossible task Ehrman suggests, especially since Ehrman himself proceeds to determine various readings throughout the book. Holding notes:

> Ehrman, as noted, has a tendency to simply create problems where none exist, and then expects readers to share his overzealous worry. Semantics dictates that his concern to have the "very words" [5] of the original, inspired text

---

[15] http://www.denverseminary.edu/dj/articles2006/0200/0206.php

is misplaced. Communication is simply not that difficult to achieve. Nor does it stand well as a claim made in a book where he claims to be solving and explaining the very things he says are problems. Furthermore, Ehrman's comments find no parallel in the works of secular textual critics, who I have yet to see say things like, "we don't have the originals" [7] or "can we be sure that all the copies were all 100 percent correct" [59] of something like Tacitus' Annals, and then make some issue over it as though it was a problem for knowing what the Annals said.[16]

Wallace has documented this argument directly from Ehrman's quotes:

…he opens chapter 7 with these words: "It is probably safe to say that the copying of early Christians texts was by and large a 'conservative' process. The scribes…were intent on 'conserving' the textual tradition they were passing on. Their ultimate concern was not to modify the tradition, but to preserve it for themselves and for those who would follow them. Most scribes, no doubt, tried to do a faithful job in making sure that the text they reproduced was the same text they inherited" (177).

"It would be a mistake…to assume that the only changes being made were by copyists with a personal stake in the wording of the text. In fact, most of the changes found in our early Christian manuscripts have nothing to do with theology or ideology. Far and away the [sic] most changes are the result of mistakes, pure and simple—slips of the pen, accidental omissions, inadvertent additions, misspelled words, blunders of one sort or another" (55).

"To be sure, of all the hundreds of thousands of changes found among the manuscripts, most of them are completely insignificant…" (207). Such concessions seem to be wrung out of him, for these facts are contrary to his agenda. In this instance, he immediately adds that "It would be wrong, however, to say—as people sometimes do—that the changes in our text have no real bearing on what the texts mean or on the theological conclusions that one draws from them" (207-8).

And he prefaces his concession by the bold statement that "The more I studied the manuscript tradition of the New Testament, the more I realized just how radically the text had been altered over the years at the hands of scribes…" (207).

But this is another claim without sufficient nuancing. Yes, scribes have changed the text, but the vast majority of changes are insignificant. And the vast majority of the rest

---

[16] http://www.tektonics.org/books/ehrqurvw.html

> are easily detectable. One almost gets the sense that it is
> the honest scholar in Ehrman who is adding these
> concessions, and the theological liberal in Ehrman who keeps
> the concessions at a minimum.[17]

At this point, some specific examples help reveal the issue. One such passage is
Acts 4:13, where Blomberg again observes:

> One surprising factual error occurs when Ehrman insists
> that Acts 4:13 means that Peter and John were illiterate
> (the term *agrammatos*—"unlettered" —in this context means not
> educated beyond the elementary education accessible to most
> first-century Jewish boys). But otherwise, the most
> disappointing feature of the volume is Ehrman's apparent
> unawareness of (or else his unwillingness to discuss) the
> difference between inductive and deductive approaches to
> Scripture. The classic evangelical formulations of
> inspiration and inerrancy have never claimed that these are
> doctrines that arise from the examination of the data of the
> existing texts. They are theological corollaries that follow
> naturally from the conviction that God is the author of the
> texts (itself suggested by 2 Tim. 3:16, Jesus' own high view
> of Scripture and his conviction that the Spirit had yet more
> truth to inspire his followers to record). But if the texts
> are "God-breathed," and if God cannot err, then they must be
> inspired and inerrant.[18]

One further disputable point regarding the picture Ehrman portrays of the early
transmission of the New Testament hinges on the idea that pre-Constantine
scribes were often semi-literate workers who included a much higher degree of
mistakes. Yet to suggest even these changes (if higher in percentage) alter the
possibility of obtaining the original text remains an unreasonable argument:

> A second supposition necessary for Ehrman's case is that
> the non-professional scribes that he postulates did most of
> the copying of New Testament documents until the fourth-
> century, when Constantine became the first emperor to
> commission new copies of the Bible, did not do nearly as
> careful a job as the professional scribes that he postulates
> did most of the post-Constantinian copying. Not only are
> both of these postulates unprovable (though certainly
> possible), the actual textual evidence of the second and
> third centuries, though notably sparser than for later
> centuries, does not demonstrate the sufficiently greater
> fluidity in the textual tradition that would be necessary to
> actually support the hypothesis that we cannot reconstruct
> the most likely originals with an exceedingly high

---

[17] http://www.bible.org/page.asp?page_id=4000
[18] http://www.denverseminary.edu/dj/articles2006/0200/0206.php

> probability of accuracy, even if that probability remains in
> the high 90s rather than at 100 %.[19]

Or, as another review highlights:

> One is rather suspicious of how Ehrman cites Celsus for
> the point that Christianity's church was "largely made up of
> the lower, uneducated classes." [41] Aside from the needed
> corrective of Meeks and Judge that Christianity early on was
> "top heavy" (relatively speaking) in the educated middle
> class, it remains that 99% of people who lived in the days
> of Celsus were of the "lower, uneducated classes" and so
> this sort of thing was merely a matter of demographic
> necessity for a movement to exist and not any sort of
> indication that the movement itself was rooted in stupidity.
> Celsus was not being honest, and Ehrman in following him is
> also not being honest, or more likely, does not have the
> needed knowledge beyond his specialty area of textual
> criticism to see his error.[20]

Finally, Ehrman provides a chapter on the little mentioned aspect of theologically and socially motivated changes in the New Testament text. However, even here his claims are primarily limited to the details that seem to support his personal views without consideration of additional options. For instance, as Blomberg points out:

> It is very helpful to understand how Mark's probable
> reference to Jesus' anger in Mark 1:41 (rather than
> compassion) fits his overall presentation of Jesus, just as
> Luke's original "omission" of Jesus sweating great drops of
> blood in the garden in Luke 24:43-44 reflects his picture of
> a more "imperturbable" Christ. Ehrman's suggestion that
> Hebrews 2:9 originally read that Christ tasted death "apart
> from God" rather than "by the grace of God" seemingly
> founders on the sheer paucity of external evidence for the
> reading. But if Origen was right that the reading stood in
> the majority of manuscripts of his day, then perhaps it was
> original. No unorthodox theology results (recall the cry of
> dereliction in the Gospels), but one can see why the vast
> majority of scribes would have adopted the reading that is
> far better known today.[21]

---

[19] http://www.denverseminary.edu/dj/articles2006/0200/0206.php
[20] http://www.tektonics.org/books/ehrqurvw.html
[21] http://www.denverseminary.edu/dj/articles2006/0200/0206.php

In summary, we find that the real New Testament may not be as difficult (or impossible) to discover as *Misquoting Jesus* suggests. As we will soon read, though evidence is provided, it is often provided from a certain slant that betrays the author's personal bias with limited concession or inclusion of differing views.

Chapter 4: Postmodern and Personal Bias in *Misquoting Jesus*

The Philly *Inquirer's* words on *Misquoting Jesus* suggest:

> But the growing religious critique argues that the Christian Nation crowd doesn't get just the Constitution wrong. It gets the Bible wrong, too.
>
> To these critics, *Misquoting Jesus* is a godsend.
>
> Ehrman, a biblical scholar, used to believe the Bible was perfect and literally true. But his scholarship taught him how flawed were the translations on which churches have built superstructures of doctrine and practice.[22]

In other words, for many skeptics, Ehrman's book provides an alternative story that fits their preconceived views on the Bible's integrity and inspiration. Each writer has his or her own personal bias, and Bart Ehrman is not immune. While those supporting his views would downplay this concept, others have noted the influence of personal bias for his arguments in *Misquoting Jesus*.

Dr. Ben Witherington, author of *The Gospel Code* and *The New Testament Story*, agrees:

> I am however glad Bart is honest about his pilgrimage. If only he could be equally honest and admit that in his scholarship he is trying now to deconstruct orthodox Christianity which he once embraced, rather than do 'value-neutral' text criticism. In my own view, he has attempted this deconstruction on the basis of very flimsy evidence—textual variants which do not prove what he wants them to prove.[23]

Ehrman himself begins his book with his own personal story, as Wallace quotes:

> "I kept reverting to my basic question: how does it help us to say that the Bible is the inerrant word of God if in fact we don't have the words that God inerrantly inspired, but only the words copied by the scribes—sometimes correctly and sometimes (many times!) incorrectly?" This is an excellent question. And it is featured prominently in *Misquoting Jesus*, being repeated throughout the book.

---

[22] http://www.philly.com/mld/inquirer/news/editorial/14297161.htm
[23] http://benwitherington.blogspot.com/2006/03/misanalyzing-text-criticism-bart.html

Unfortunately, Ehrman does not really spend much time wrestling with it directly.

"The Bible," Ehrman notes, "began to appear to me as a very human book… This was a human book from beginning to end."

"It is a radical shift from reading the Bible as an inerrant blueprint for our faith, life, and future to seeing it as a very human book… This is the shift in my own thinking that I ended up making, and to which I am now fully committed."[24]

The most intriguing work in this regard, however, has not emerged from a theologian's study, but rather from an unusually personal article featured in the *Washington Post*. Here, the writer narrates:

He attended Trinity Episcopal on Vermont Street in Lawrence, but he and his family were casual in their faith. Lost in the middle of the pack in school, Ehrman felt an emptiness settle over him, something that lingered at nights after the lights were out, when the house was quiet.

One afternoon he went to a party at the house of a popular kid. It turned out to be a meeting of a Christian outreach youth group from a nearby college. In private talks, the charismatic young leader of the group told the 15-year-old Ehrman that the emptiness he felt inside was nothing less than his soul crying out for God. He quoted Scripture to prove it.

"Given my reverence for, but ignorance of, the Bible, it all sounded completely convincing," Ehrman writes.

One Saturday morning after having breakfast with the man, Ehrman went home, walked into his room and closed the door. He knelt by his bed and asked the Lord to come into his life.

He rose, and felt better, stronger. "It was your bona fide born-again experience."

The void in his heart was filled. The more he read the Bible, he says, the closer he felt to God.

His devotion soon engulfed him. "I told my friends, family, everyone about Christ," he remembers now. "The study of the Bible was a religious experience. The more you studied the Bible, the more spiritual you were. I memorized

---

[24] http://www.bible.org/page.asp?page_id=4000

```
large parts of it. It was a spiritual exercise, like
meditation."²⁵
```

However, as this same article and introduction to *Misquoting Jesus* points out, life drastically changed during his college years. After studying the Greek text of the New Testament at Evangelical schools Moody Bible Institute and Wheaton College, Ehrman chose to pursue M.Div. and PhD. degrees from Princeton Theological Seminary. Here, he studied under Bruce Metzger, North America's premier authority on New Testament textual criticism.

During his studies, he also encountered professors who held very different views regarding the Bible's accuracy and transmission:

```
He wrote a tortured paper at Princeton that sought to
explain how an episode in Mark might be true, despite clear
evidence to the contrary. A professor wrote in the margin:

"Maybe Mark just made a mistake."

As simple as it was, it struck him to the core.

"The evidence for the belief is that if you look closely
at the Bible, at the resurrection, you'll find the evidence
for it," he says. "For me, that was the seed of its own
destruction. It wasn't there. It isn't there."

"I just began to lose it," Ehrman says now, in a
conversation that stretches from late afternoon into the
evening. "It wasn't for lack of trying. But I just couldn't
believe there was a God in charge of this mess . . . It was
so emotionally charged. This whole business of 'the Bible is
your life, and anyone who doesn't believe it is going to
roast in hell.'"²⁶
```

The saga continued. After several years of teaching religious studies at the University of North Carolina, he now claims to be a "happy agnostic." That emptiness he felt as a teenager is still there, but he fills it with family, friends, work and the finer things in life.

---

[25] Neely Tucker, "The Book of Bart: In the Bestseller 'Misquoting Jesus,' Agnostic Author Bart Ehrman Picks Apart the Gospels That Made a Disbeliever Out of Him," *Washington Post*, March 5, 2006. Accessed at http://www.washingtonpost.com/wp-dyn/content/article/2006/03/04/ AR2006030401369.html

[26] *Ibid.*

> "He thinks that when you die, there are no Pearly Gates. 'I think you just cease to exist, like the mosquito you swatted yesterday.'"[27]

Three decades later, the God-honoring young Ehrman has turned agnostic. In the writer's words, "What he found in the ancient papyri of the scriptorium was not the greatest story ever told, but the crumbling dust of his own faith."[28]

Perhaps the best summary of how Ehrman's personal beliefs drive his writing in *Misquoting Jesus* comes in the form of a question. In the same *Washington Post* article, Dr. Darrell Bock is quoted as saying:

> "I think Bart is writing about his personal journey, about legitimate things that bother him," says Darrell Bock, research professor of New Testament studies at the Dallas Theological Seminary. Like many Christian scholars who have studied the ancient scrolls, Bock says his faith was strengthened by the same process that destroyed Ehrman's.
>
> "Even if I don't have a high-definition photograph of the empty tomb to prove Christ's resurrection, there's the reaction to something after Christ died that is very hard to explain away," Bock says. "There was no resurrection tradition in Jewish theology. Where did it come from? How did these illiterate, impoverished fishermen create such a powerful religion?[29]

---

[27] *Ibid.*

[28] *Ibid.*

[29] *Ibid.*

Chapter 5: Quantity of Manuscript Changes vs. Quality of Changes

New Testament textual criticism can be defined as identifying variations among manuscripts and working to determine which variation is most likely original. One major contention lies with how to determine the importance of manuscripts based on the *quantity* of manuscripts (how many exist) versus the *quality* of manuscripts (earlier age and integrity).

In *Misquoting Jesus*, Ehrman tackles these issues in Chapter 3 "Texts of the New Testament" and Chapter 4 "The Quest for Origins." Here, he rightly points out some of the errors of the edited text of Erasmus, especially noting his faulty Latin-to-Greek back translations for portions of Revelation and dependence on later Byzantine manuscripts.

He also discusses the role of Bengel, highlighting his careful research on New Testament variations. Even at this point, however, his storytelling is selective, as Wallace notes:

> But even here, Ehrman injects his own viewpoint by his selection of material. For example, in discussing the role that Bengel played in the history of textual criticism (109-112), Ehrman gives this pious German conservative high praise as a scholar: he was an "extremely careful interpreter of the biblical text" (109); "Bengel studied everything intensely" (111). Ehrman speaks about Bengel's breakthroughs in textual criticism (111-12), *but does not mention that he was the first important scholar to articulate the doctrine of the orthodoxy of the variants.* This is a curious omission because, on the one hand, Ehrman is well aware of this fact, for in the fourth edition of *The Text of the New Testament*, now by Bruce Metzger and Bart Ehrman, which appeared just months before *Misquoting Jesus*, the authors note, "With characteristic energy and perseverance, [Bengel] procured all the editions, manuscripts, and early translations available to him. After extended study, he came to the conclusions that the variant readings were fewer in number than might have been expected and that they did not shake any article of evangelic doctrine." (emphasis added)[30]

While the brevity of *Misquoting Jesus* may require less interaction with certain issues, it is intriguing that there is so little emphasis on the external evidence of

---

[30] http://www.bible.org/page.asp?page_id=4000

New Testament manuscripts in these chapters. In seeking information on individual manuscripts, the reader can find extremely little in chapters where one would expect to find such discussion.

In the battle of quantity of manuscripts versus quality, Ehrman appears to depend strongly on manuscript quality for his arguments, pushing the quantity issue to a level that blurs one's view of how to handle differing manuscript variations:

> Ehrman overplays the quality of the variants while underscoring their quantity. He says, "There are more variations among our manuscripts than there are words in the New Testament." Elsewhere he states that the number of variants is as high as 400,000. That is true enough, but by itself is misleading. Anyone who teaches NT textual criticism knows that this fact is only part of the picture and that, if left dangling in front of the reader without explanation, is a distorted view. Once it is revealed that the great majority of these variants are inconsequential—involving spelling differences that cannot even be translated, articles with proper nouns, word order changes, and the like—and that only a very small minority of the variants alter the meaning of the text, the whole picture begins to come into focus. Indeed, only about 1% of the textual variants are both meaningful and viable. The impression Ehrman sometimes gives throughout the book—and repeats in interviews—is that of wholesale uncertainty about the original wording, a view that is far more radical than he actually embraces.[31]

At this point in the dialogue, a compilation of some of the book's quotes helps to point out the flow of Ehrman's message. Consider the following:

- "Our manuscripts are...full of mistakes" (57).

- "Not only do we not have the originals, we don't have the first copies of the originals. We don't even have copies of the copies of the originals, or copies of the copies of the copies of the originals. What we have are copies made later—much later...And these copies all differ from one another, in many thousands of places... these copies differ from one another in so many places that we don't even known how many differences there are" (10).

---

[31] Wallace article.

- "Mistakes multiply and get repeated; sometimes they get corrected and sometimes they get compounded. And so it goes. For centuries" (57).

- "We could go on nearly forever talking about specific places in which the texts of the New Testament came to be changed, either accidentally or intentionally. As I have indicated, the examples are not just in the hundreds but in the thousands" (98).

- "To the shock and dismay of many of his readers, Mill's apparatus isolated some thirty thousand places of variation among the surviving witnesses... Mill was not exhaustive in his presentation of the data he had collected. He had, in fact, found far more than thirty thousand places of variation" (84).

- "Scholars differ significantly in their estimates—some say there are 200,000 variants known, some say 300,000, some say 400,000 or more! We do not know for sure because, despite impressive developments in computer technology, no one has yet been able to count them all" (89)

- "[Mark 16:9-20 and John 7:53-8:11] represent just two out of thousands of places in which the manuscripts of the New Testament came to be changed by scribes" (68).[32]

The compounding effect of these types of blanket statements is that the everyday reader could find themselves assuming the sheer number of differences means the text itself is completely inaccurate and impossible to determine. Granted, Ehrman does offer the occasional disclaimer. For instance, he states on page 69 that, "Although most of the changes are not of this magnitude, there are lots of significant changes (and lots more insignificant ones)..." Such concessions, however, seem to be somewhat misleading.

As another review observes:

> But this sounds as if there are at least a few others that are of similar size, when in fact there are no other

---

[32] Special thanks to Daniel Wallace for identifying the quotes discussed in this section.

> textual variants anywhere that are even one-fourth as long
> as these thirteen- and twelve-verse additions.[33]

One further writer has noted an issue that strikes the discerning reader as disturbing:

> Ehrman's thesis seems to hinge on the belief that we can
> know which passages were changed, even while we have no
> confidence in the original text. This is, quite simply,
> untenable. His thesis also casts doubt on all of ancient
> history, for surely the problems with transmission of
> documents is not unique to Christianity (even if, as he
> suggests, it is particularly pronounced among those who used
> amateur scribes).[34]

The idea that a quantity of differences offers proof of error seems more intended to alarm readers rather than to deal with specific variations. While arguments are made regarding some of the classic Bible texts that remain in dispute (such as the longer ending of Mark and John's story of the woman caught in adultery), the statistics are thrown in with a couple of other easy targets, giving readers the idea that there are several more the chapter simply didn't allow space to include. Readers should be aware that the arguments discussed in *Misquoting Jesus* are the extremes rather than the norm and that no major theological beliefs rise or fall with either conclusion.

---

[33] http://www.denverseminary.edu/dj/articles2006/0200/0206.php.
[34] http://www.dietofbookworms.com/title.php?id=594, book review.

Chapter 6: Deal or No Deal: Must Inerrancy Be All or Nothing?

On page 248 of *Misquoting Jesus*, we read, "It would be wrong…to say—as people sometimes do—that the changes in our text have no real bearing on what the texts mean or on the theological conclusions that one draws from them. We have seen, in fact, that just the opposite is the case."

Beginning in Chapter 5, Ehrman begins his more controversial aspects of his work, largely a simplified version of his scholarly-level research provided in his Oxford release, *The Orthodox Corruption of Scripture*. By the end of Chapter 7, the reader is offered a fuller insight into the perspective Ehrman promotes.

Two specific issues are argued regarding the Evangelical view of inerrancy. The first is the view that since we do not have the originals of the New Testament manuscripts, then inerrancy is invalid. However, as we have previously discussed, if such standards were strictly applied, all historical documents would be questionable. For instance, no originals of Homer's *Iliad* remain nor of the works of Socrates, yet these works are not questioned at the level of the New Testament, though they are much older and based on fewer manuscripts. Wallace's words summarize this argument well:

> Regardless of what one thinks about the doctrine of inerrancy, the argument against it on the basis of the unknown autographs is logically fallacious. This is so for two reasons. First, we have the text of the NT somewhere in the manuscripts. There is no need for conjecture, except perhaps in one or two places. Second, the text we have in any viable variants is no more a problem for inerrancy than other problems where the text is secure. Now, to be sure, there are some challenges in the textual variants to inerrancy. This is not denied. But there are simply bigger fish to fry when it comes to issues that inerrancy faces. Thus, if conjectural emendation is unnecessary, and if no viable variant registers much of a blip on the radar called 'problems for inerrancy,' then not having the originals is a moot point for this doctrine. It's not a moot point for verbal inspiration, of course, but it is for inerrancy.[35]

The second argument Ehrman argues is that variants in the manuscripts change the foundational theology of the New Testament. For instance, his summary on page 208 states:

---

[35] http://www.bible.org/page.asp?page_id=4000

> In some instances, the very meaning of the text is at
> stake, depending on how one resolves a textual problem: Was
> Jesus an angry man [Mark 1.41]? Was he completely distraught
> in the face of death [Heb 2.8-9]? Did he tell his disciples
> that they could drink poison without being harmed [Mark
> 16.9-20]? Did he let an adulteress off the hook with nothing
> but a mild warning [John 7.53-8.11]? Is the doctrine of the
> Trinity explicitly taught in the New Testament [1 John 5.7-
> 8]? Is Jesus actually called "the unique God" there [John
> 1.18]? Does the New Testament indicate that even the Son of
> God himself does not know when the end will come [Matt
> 24.36]? The questions go on and on, and all of them are
> related to how one resolves difficulties in the manuscript
> tradition as it has come down to us.

The three specific passages presented for this conclusion include the longer
ending of Mark, the adulterous woman in John's Gospel, and 1 John 5:7-8.
Numerous problems emerge from this argument once we begin studying these
passages.

The Longer Ending of Mark

Ehrman's treatment of the controversial ending of Mark appears to prove the
passage is not only unauthentic, but rather the tip of the iceberg regarding New
Testament textual problems. However, several unmentioned issues soften his
book's concerns on this issue.

First, nearly all Evangelical textual scholars agree that the longer ending of
Mark was not original. A simple glance at today's modern translations will
reveal most contain a footnote stating this fact. However, because this longer
ending was included in the King James Version and this version has had such an
enduring impact on English-speaking cultures, even the most contemporary
translations refuse to remove the verses altogether.

Second, regardless of which ending is accurate, there is no major issue of
theology at stake. Unless one holds that snakes handling or drinking poison are
essential components of one's Christian faith, there is nothing in Mark 16:9-20
that undermines the beliefs of the Christian faith. In fact, three major views are
offered in the notes of the NET Bible translation on the real ending of Mark.
None of the three options cause a problem for Christian readers. "There are three
possible explanations for Mark ending at 16:8: (1) The author intentionally ended

the Gospel here in an open-ended fashion; (2) the Gospel was never finished; or (3) the last leaf of the ms [manuscript] was lost prior to copying."[36]

Third, the issue of inerrancy does not rise or fall on the longer ending of Mark. If the final verses are unoriginal, then they are uninspired material later added to the story. If they were original (which is highly doubtful), then they are inspired words and primarily confirm the accounts provided in the other gospels.

What Ehrman does rightly note in regard to this account is that there were times when copyists added material intentionally throughout the history of the New Testament's transmission. However, even in this case, the original material can be determined with a high degree of accuracy, meaning an Evangelical view of inerrancy can exist with or without Mark's longer ending.

The Adulterous Woman in John 7:53-8:11

Similarly, Ehrman also provides the evidence behind the likely scenario that John 7:53-8:11 is a later edition to John's Gospel. In 1988, Ehrman wrote a well-researched journal article on this same set of verses showing that this story is most likely a combined account of two different historical encounters rather than an original New Testament account.[37] Whether or not one is inclined to agree with this exact interpretation, even conservative scholars agree that the external evidence for the account provides little evidence for its inclusion as an original passage:

> In retrospect, keeping these two pericopae [stories] in our Bibles rather than relegating them to the footnotes seems to have been a bomb just waiting to explode. All Ehrman did was to light the fuse. One lesson we must learn from *Misquoting Jesus* is that those in ministry need to close the gap between the church and the academy. We have to educate believers. Instead of trying to isolate laypeople from critical scholarship, we need to insulate them. They need to be ready for the barrage, because it is coming… The intentional dumbing down of the church for the sake of filling more pews will ultimately lead to defection from Christ. Ehrman is to be thanked for giving us a wake-up call.[38]

---

[36] Mark 16:9, Footnote 9, www.netbible.com.
[37] Bart D. Ehrman, "Jesus and the Adulteress," *NTS* 34 (1988) 24-44.
[38] http://www.bible.org/page.asp?page_id=4000.

Though strong words for the contemporary Church, the statement clearly indicates the need for informed teaching on such historically controversial passages that some will use to disregard the Bible's integrity.

1 John 5:7-8 and the Trinitarian Formula

First, it must be noted that modern translations do not include this passage, acknowledging for centuries the inaccuracy of its usage. For this reason alone, it is curious why *Misquoting Jesus* even invests such time on these verses.

The motivation may be to further strengthen Ehrman's argument for a Bible changed through political force. In this instance, he is correct. He rightly notes that the verse did not even enter the Bible until 1522. Even at the time, those working with the text knew it was inauthentic. Ehrman's account provides the highlights of this story:

> As the story goes, Erasmus—possibly in an unguarded moment—agreed that he would insert the verse in a future edition of his Greek New Testament on one condition: that his opponents produce a Greek manuscript in which the verse could be found (finding it in Latin manuscripts was not enough). And so a Greek manuscript was produced. In fact, it was produced for the occasion...Despite his misgivings, Erasmus was true to his word and included the Johannine Comma in his next edition, and in all his subsequent editions...And so familiar passages to readers of the English Bible—form the King James in 1611 onward, up until modern editions of the twentieth century—include the woman taken in adultery, the last twelve verses of Mark, and the Johannine Comma, eve though none of these passages can be found in the oldest and superior manuscripts of the Greek New Testament.[39]

While this verse's history definitely fuels Ehrman's viewpoint, it simply highlights a historical problem translators have long corrected. To suggest that this error disproves the Trinity or the original manuscript's inerrancy is a logical fallacy. Does one historical flaw mean the entire New Testament is flawed? It would be the equivalent of saying that because my toe is broken, that my entire body is useless. The greater (my body) controls the lesser (my toe), not the other way around, regardless of how it pains my walking. In the same way, a flaw in one point of the New Testament's text does not necessarily mean the entire New Testament is flawed.

---

[39] *Misquoting Jesus*, p. 81-82.

Additionally, is this the only statement regarding the three parts of the Trinity in the New Testament? While it may be the clearest statement, there are several other verses that could provide the evidence behind this issue. Certainly this was the case, since church fathers long before 1522 explicitly affirmed their biblically based belief regarding the Orthodox view of the Trinity.

However, one could argue inerrancy's integrity is questionable even if one place is inaccurate. I would agree, but with this disclaimer. In none of the above cases is there a situation in which the original text is not one of the options, meaning inerrancy can still stand depending on the view one takes. This is where faith (or lack thereof) influences one's bias on these issues. For Ehrman, what is seen as "mistakes" indicates a flawed document and therefore no inerrancy. For another (such as myself), a mistake offers the possibility for further study into *which* option is the right option, seeking the true words of the text because of my theological beliefs in inerrancy.

Again, one wonders why this passage is even discussed in Ehrman's book. The only reason seems to be to fuel doubts. The passage made its way into our Bibles through political pressure, appearing for the first time in 1522, even though scholars then and now knew that it was not authentic.

As Blomberg notes in his conservative review in the *Denver Journal*:

> Ehrman offers no supporting arguments for his claims that if God inspired the originals, he both could have and should have inerrantly preserved them in all subsequent copies. It would have been a far greater miracle to supernaturally guide every copyist and translator throughout history than to inspire one set of original authors, and in the process it probably would have violated the delicate balance between the humanity and divinity of the Bible analogous to the humanity and divinity of Christ. All that is necessary is for us to have reason to believe that we can reconstruct something remarkably close to the originals, and we have evidence for that in abundance. No central tenet of Christianity hangs on any textually uncertain passage; this observation alone means that Christian textual critics may examine the variants that do exist dispassionately and without worrying that their faith is somehow threatened in the ways that Ehrman came to believe.[40]

Though this dives into a separate issue, the theme is that the view of inerrancy does not hinge on these debated texts. Those reading *Misquoting Jesus* would do well to understand these issues when considering its claims.

---

[40] http://www.denverseminary.edu/dj/articles2006/0200/0206.php

Chapter 7: New Testament: Remix or Remake?

In a *Dallas Morning News* interview, Dr. Ehrman was quoted as saying regarding the New Testament that:

> "Most of the differences don't matter, but some of the differences are huge," said Bart Ehrman, chairman of the department of religious studies at the University of North Carolina and the author of *Misquoting Jesus*, a book that suggests sections of the New Testament were changed over the early centuries of Christianity.
>
> Dr. Ehrman admits, however, that no major tenet of mainstream Christianity rests solely on disputed texts. Most of the details in the disputed last verses of Mark, for example, are found elsewhere in the New Testament.
>
> But original versions of some passages support different interpretations of the nature and mission of Jesus, he said.
>
> "In some instances, the choice affects the meaning of an entire passage, or even an entire book," he said.
>
> For example, in *Misquoting Jesus*, he cites Luke's account of John baptizing Jesus. Modern translations have God saying, "You are my beloved son in whom I am well pleased." But Dr. Ehrman says the original said something quite different: "You are my son. Today I have begotten you."[41]

The *Dallas Morning News* is not alone in providing newsprint for Dr. Ehrman's views regarding what could be called a "remake" of the New Testament. A simple online search provides well over a dozen national newspapers that have provided reviews highlighting his bestselling work.

Yet does Ehrman's questioning of a New Testament with intentionally changed words stand up under evaluation? In *Misquoting Jesus*, he addresses issues with the "angry" Jesus, changes in the healing accounts of the gospels,

---

[41] http://www.dallasnews.com/sharedcontent/dws/news/localnews/stories/DN-biblesays_16rel.ART.State.Edition2.3e66907.html

and issues regarding women. Women's issues will be handled in a later chapter, but we will discuss the other two areas here.

The "Angry" Jesus

In addressing textual variants in the New Testament manuscripts that have theological implications, Ehrman specifically discusses the idea of the anger of Jesus:

> In some instances, the very meaning of the text is at stake, depending on how one resolves a textual problem: Was Jesus an angry man [Mark 1.41]? Was he completely distraught in the face of death [Heb 2.8-9]? Did he tell his disciples that they could drink poison without being harmed [Mark 16.9-20]? Did he let an adulteress off the hook with nothing but a mild warning [John 7.53-8.11]? Is the doctrine of the Trinity explicitly taught in the New Testament [1 John 5.7-8]? Is Jesus actually called "the unique God" there [John 1.18]? Does the New Testament indicate that even the Son of God himself does not know when the end will come [Matt 24.36]? The questions go on and on, and all of them are related to how one resolves difficulties in the manuscript tradition as it has come down to us. (pg. 208)

However, his details on this argument seek to prove too much. For instance, he quickly dismisses any varying arguments regarding Mark 1:41. As Wallace observes:

> Ehrman's dismissal of all alternative interpretations to his understanding of why and at whom Jesus was angry in Mark 1.41 is too cavalier. His certitude that "even the commentators who realize that the text originally indicated that Jesus became angry are embarrassed by the idea and try to explain it away, so that the text no longer means what it says" ("A Leper in the Hands of an Angry Jesus," 86) implies that his interpretation surely must be right. (Although Ehrman makes quick work of various views, he does not interact at all with Proctor's view, apparently because he was unaware of Proctor's dissertation when he wrote his piece for the Hawthorne Festschrift. Proctor essentially argues that the healing of the leper is a double healing, which also implicitly involves an exorcism ["A Case for the Angry Jesus," 312-16]. Proctor summarizes his argument as follows: "Given (1) popular first-century views regarding the link between demons and disease, (2) the exorcistic language of v 43, (3) the behavior of demoniacs and those associated with them elsewhere in the Gospel, and (4) Luke's treatment of Mark 1:29-31, this seems to be a relatively safe assumption even though Mark makes [sic] does not explicitly describe the man as a demoniac" [325-26, n. 6].)

Not only does Ehrman charge exegetes with misunderstanding
Mark's ὀργισθείς, he also says that Matthew and Luke don't
understand: "[A]nyone not intimately familiar with Mark's
Gospel on its own terms… may not have understood why Jesus
became angry. Matthew certainly did not; neither did Luke"
(ibid., 98). Is it not perhaps a bit too brash to claim that
the reason Matthew and Luke dropped *orgistheiv* was because
they were ignorant of Mark's purposes? After all, were they
not also 'intimately familiar with Mark's Gospel'? Are there
not any other plausible reasons for their omission?

This dialogue alone shows that at least some have directly dealt with this verse's controversy rather than trying to hide or cover up an accurate interpretation, as Ehrman has suggested.

Furthermore, his discussion suggests that the theme of compassion is not shown in Mark's gospel to prove Ehrman's point. However, it is important to note that in every instance in Mark where anger is shown in the life of Jesus, it is regarding a healing account. Mark 3:5 provides the example of Jesus' frustration with the people who were waiting to see if he would heal someone on the Sabbath. The surrounding verses (Mark 3:4-6) reveal the background:

Then Jesus asked them, "Which is lawful on the Sabbath:
to do good or to do evil, to save life or to kill?" But they
remained silent. He looked around at them in anger and,
deeply distressed at their stubborn hearts, said to the man,
"Stretch out your hand." He stretched it out, and his hand
was completely restored. Then the Pharisees went out and
began to plot with the Herodians how they might kill Jesus
(NIV).

In this example, Jesus is clearly upset with the Pharisees (v. 6) who were more concerned about catching him doing "work" on the Sabbath than in a person in need of healing. Yes, Jesus is angry here. However, his anger is just, based on helping someone in need.

The Healings of Jesus

Ehrman's treatment of Mark 1:30-31 stands out as particularly odd. In this healing account of Peter's mother-in-law, he notes that her healing should not necessarily be considered an example of compassion. He specifically notes, "The only story in this opening chapter of Mark that hints at personal compassion is the healing of Simon Peter's mother-in-law, sick in bed. But even that compassionate interpretation may be open to question. Some wry observers have noted that after Jesus dispels her fever, she rises to serve them, presumably bringing them their evening meal" (p. 138).

He then argues that Jesus is presented in Mark as a "powerful figure with a strong will and an agenda of his own, a charismatic authority who doesn't like to be disturbed" (p. 138). But could there be another interpretation for this healing account? Wouldn't her return to the everyday duties of the time be understood by readers as proof of her complete healing? Other biblical examples provide similar physical reinforcement of miraculous deeds, such as Jesus eating a piece of fish after his resurrection as evidence of his physical return (Luke 24:41-43), Lazarus eating with Jesus after coming back to life four days after his death (John 11:42-12:2), and the synagogue ruler's daughter restored to life (Mark 5:42).[42]

Many of these healings necessarily include the idea of compassion as well, another concept *Misquoting Jesus* argues against. Wallace notes the weaknesses of this approach:

> Third, in more than one healing narrative in the synoptic Gospels—including the healing of Peter's mother-in-law—we see strong hints of compassion on Jesus' part when he grabs the person's hand. In Matt 9.25; Mark 1.31; 5.41; 9.27; and Luke 8.54 the expression each time is κρατήσας/ἐκράτησεν τῆς χειρός. *Krateno* with a genitive direct object, rather than an accusative direct object, is used in these texts. In the Gospels when this verb takes an accusative direct object, it has the force of seizing, clinging to, holding firmly (cf. Matt 14.3; 21.46; 22.6; 26.57; 28.9; Mark 6.17; 7.3, 4, 8; but when it takes a genitive direct object, it implies a gentle touch more than a firm grip, and is used only in healing contexts (note the translation in the NET of κρατήσας/ἐκράτησεν τῆς χειρός in Matt 9.25; Mark 1.31; 5.41; 9.27; and Luke 8.54). What is to be noted in these texts is not only that there is no difference between Mark on the one hand and Matthew and Luke on the other, but that Mark actually has more instances of this idiom than Matthew and Luke combined. How does this 'gently taking her/him by the hand' not speak of compassion?[43]

Further examples could be noted, but the idea that the healings of Jesus are something "remade" or "remixed" through the process of transmission through the centuries cannot stand as strongly as Ehrman claims. While time and

---

[42] Yes, these are all accounts of people coming back to life from the dead, but certainly count as healing stories as well.

[43] http://www.bible.org/page.asp?page_id=4000.

29

multiplication of texts certainly allows for such errors, the vast majority of texts agree to such an extent that a claim for theologically-motivated changes to our Bibles today should not scare today's reader.

Undoing His Undoing

One of the more intriguing comments Ehrman makes on interpretation in general occurs near the end of his book. On page 217 he provides an insightfully postmodern note that appears to undo his own interpretations on theologically-motivated changes in the New Testament:

> "The only way to make sense of a text is to read it, and the only way to read it is by putting it in other words, and the only way to put it in other words is by having other words to put it into, and the only way you have other words to put it into is that you have a life, and the only way to have a life is by being filled with desires, longings, needs, wants, beliefs, perspectives, worldviews, opinions, likes, dislikes—and all the other things that make human beings human. *And so to read a text, necessarily, is to change a text*" (emphasis added).

If I understand him correctly, these words appear to state that every reader of the text will bring away a different interpretation. This being the case, there will be no consistent or common understanding of the text because individual bias will not allow for a fair and neutral reading. While this worldview itself is debatable, the conclusion for our discussion is that it would seem to make no difference whether the text was changed or not. In the end, the reader is the one deciding what is true or untrue.

Dr. Darrell Bock's words on this issue are worthy of reflection:

> The fact that a few scribes "misquoted" certain words does not mean the Bible we have today is filled with misquotations. When it is translated from the mass of manuscripts and on the basis of each text's contextual argument, the Bible is consistent, stable, and faithful to its original meaning. Ehrman makes a valid point about individual cases in verses here and there, but that should not lead us to believe that our Bible today is a distortion of the original.[44]

For Evangelical Christians, we would do well to note this influence in *Misquoting Jesus*. The Bible declares itself as truth from God. In a very objective way, we

---

[44]http://www.beliefnet.com/story/188/story_18803_1.html

affirm that its words are true and that differing view cannot necessarily also be true. In other words, either two plus two equal four or it does not. We cannot say both options are true or that neither option is true. We must make a choice.

In the present case, the truth is that the New Testament's transmission has been influenced throughout history, but that enough copies exist to help us determine the original wording in nearly all cases and apply those words as Christians accordingly.

Chapter 8: Misquoting Jesus and the King James Only Debate

> "That is the kind of book this is—to my knowledge, the
> first of its kind. It is written for people who know nothing
> about textual criticism but who might like to learn
> something about how scribes were changing scripture and
> about how we can recognize where they did so." (*Misquoting
> Jesus*, p. 15)

According to the author himself, *Misquoting Jesus* is the first book written from this particular perspective. While this may be true in the specific sense he defines, it is important to note that the past century has included several works on this issue by those holding to a "King James-only" view of scripture.[45]

Among King James-only advocates, one of the central criticisms is that modern Bible translations distort or "water down" the literal words of the Bible as translated by the King James Version. On this issue, Ehrman provides very convincing evidence that much earlier and better manuscripts have been discovered since the 1611 release of this historic English translation that have helped readers better understand the original words of the New Testament.

In fact, some of the arguments discussed in earlier chapters of *Misquotes in Misquoting Jesus* fall in Ehrman's *favor* for those holding only to the King James Version, but fail to convince when including more modern translations. For instance, the Trinitarian formula argument in 1 John 5:7-8 is included in the King James (and New King James) but not in the NIV, NASB, NLT, or other modern versions. Even most study Bibles based on the King James or New King James note this difference. One recent bestselling study Bible, the NKJV MacArthur Study Bible by Dr. John MacArthur, states the following "disclaimer" on these verses:

> These words are a direct reference to the Trinity and
> what they say is accurate. External manuscript evidence,
> however, is against them being in the original epistle… Most
> likely, the words were added much later to the text.[46]

On the flip side, it must also be noted that Ehrman's near attack on the King James Version toward the end of his book shows an emotionally-charged and

---

[45] For instance, the web ministry at http://www.kjvonly.org/bookstore.htm includes several such books.

[46] John MacArthur, Jr., *The MacArthur Study Bible*.

exaggerated approach to the enduring value of the positive benefits of the King James translation. For instance, he writes on page 209:

> The King James Version is filled with places in which the translators rendered a Greek text derived ultimately from Erasmus's edition, which was based on a single twelfth-century manuscript that is one of the worst of the manuscripts we now have available to us! It's no wonder that modern translations often differ from the King James, and no wonder that some Bible-believing Christians prefer to pretend there's never a problem, since God inspired the King James Bible instead of the original Greek! (As the old saying goes, If the King James was good enough for Saint Paul, it's good enough for me.)
>
> Reality is never that neat, however, and in this case we need to face up to the facts. The King James was not given by God but was a translation by as group of scholars in the early seventeenth century who based heir rendition on a faulty Greek text.

Despite the portion of truth contained in his comments, the King James preface itself points out the real attitude of those scholars involved in its making. The following words come directly from the opening of the 1611 version (with modernized spellings):

> "...it hath pleased God in his divine providence, here and there to scatter words and sentences of that difficulty and doubtfulness, not in doctrinal points that concern salvation, (for in such it hath been vouched that the Scriptures are plain) but in matters of less moment, that fearfulness would better beseem us than confidence..."
>
> "But we desire that the Scripture may speak like itself, as in the language of Canaan, that it may be understood even of the very vulgar."[47]

It seems clear, then, that though the King James version is an easy target four hundred years after its making, its authors carried an attitude of humility and a desire to learn of any new information that would help in better translating and understanding the Bible.

Two specific textual problems remain from the later chapters of *Misquoting Jesus* in which the King James Version impacts the argument.[48] Though originally

---

[47] Modern –spelling citations from http://www.tegart.com/brian/bible/kjvonly/transaid.html.

stated by Wallace, I have shared these in relation to how the King James influences our understanding and Ehrman's arguments.

Hebrews 2:8-9

The NIV states regarding the end of verse nine: "…so that by the grace of God he might taste death for everyone." Some variants instead word the ending as saying, "apart from God" in place of "the grace of God." Ehrman argues "apart from God" as original.[49]

The conclusion he makes is that this "original reading" changes orthodox or traditional theology because it claims Jesus died on the cross "apart from God," making Jesus more human and separate from God the Father.

Several thoughts, however, remain unanswered. First, how can this verse claim such a human view of Jesus (in Ehrman's view) when verse 8 quotes Psalm 8:4-6 in which the reference talks of all (created) things living in subjection to the Messiah, Jesus?

Second, how can Ehrman prove the impact of the change regarding this verse? In other words, if he is correct, how is the reading, "…more consistent with the theology of Hebrews."[50] His discussion does not demonstrate how (or if) this is the case.

Third, how does this change alter any major portion of New Testament theology? If the change he suggests is correct, does it really prove that scribes intentionally changed the wording or rather that this is a difficult text to interpret based on the variations? Regardless of how the phrase was originally worded, how is a Bible-believing person's faith actually different? The cause-effect relationship suggested does not seem to be as life-changing as *Misquoting Jesus* presses.

In relationship to the King James Version, it is interesting to note that its translation stands consistent with the consensus of scholars on modern translations as well. In this instance, the four hundred year time span has not

---

[48] John 1:18 is also argued, but is not discussed here. See Wallace's argument for the Greek manuscript issues here at http://www.bible.org/page.asp?page_id=4000.

[49] Again, how he can argue what is original after claiming the original wording cannot be determined is a circular argument, but this section only addresses this specific verse rather than his overall approach.

[50] *Misquoting Jesus*, p. 132.

provided manuscript evidence to persuade the majority of Bible translators (of any kind of background) to accept a different position.

Matthew 24:36

Matthew 24:36 states that even the Son does not know when the time of his return would be, but only the Father. The King James translates: "But of that day and hour knoweth no man, no, not the angels of heaven, but my Father only." Some manuscripts also include in this verse the phrase "nor the Son." Was this an original part of the verse or a later scribal tradition?

Among textual critics, this is seen as a genuinely controversial point. The manuscript tradition does contain copies listing both views. What strikes me as interesting is Ehrman's degree of certainty on his decision on the issue. The controversy here surrounds how this change would alter one's view of Jesus. Would the change require that Jesus is somehow more human and therefore impact our beliefs about Jesus?

Certainly, the idea that Jesus does not know something could alter evangelical theology's view that Jesus knows all things. However, to claim this with certainty is misleading. Plus, even if Ehrman is correct on the text's original wording (though not conclusively proven), he does not clearly demonstrate how this could harmonize with the rest of the New Testament's words about Jesus. For instance, could it be possible that Jesus would "choose" not to know when he would return in order to provide a sense of expectancy among his followers and those still seeking? This should at least be considered as an alternative possibility. Yet Ehrman seems to dismiss other options here in order to press his point. Whether to fit an abbreviated book length or to mislead readers is not something that can be determined, but readers certainly are directed to see only one view here rather than the difficulties involved in determining and interpreting the original text.[51]

What Dr. Gordon Fee states of Ehrman's *Orthodox Corruption of Scripture*[52] continues to apply to the textual arguments in *Misquoting Jesus*, especially in relation to its discussion to the King James version. "Unfortunately, Ehrman too often turns mere *possibility* into *probability*, and probability into *certainty*, where

---

[51] See www.netbible.com notes on this verse for the particular Greek manuscript evidence presented from an Evangelical perspective.
[52] Seen in many reviews as the academic version upon which much of *Misquoting Jesus* was based.

other equally viable reasons for corruption exist."[53] Those either of the King James persuasion or otherwise can learn from Ehrman's historical notes, but should continue to be aware of additional perspectives avoided or quickly dismissed in the discussions of *Misquoting Jesus*.

---

[53] Gordon D. Fee, *The Orthodox Corruption of Scripture* in Critical Review of *Books in Religion* 8 (1995) 204.

Chapter 9: Women's Issues in *Misquoting Jesus*

Ehrman notes that the Bible is not the word of God but the word of man. The work of many men and no women, who spent the better part of 20 centuries combing over the teachings of Jesus and his disciples to make them conform with accepted church doctrine.[54]

Beginning on page 178, *Misquoting Jesus* focuses on "Women and the Texts of Scripture." He begins well. For instance, he rightly notes that, "…it is clear that even after his death, Jesus's message continued to be attractive to women."[55] Later, he writes, "Women, in short, appear to have played a significant role in the churches of Paul's day."[56]

However, his argument at points spiral beyond to additional areas. In one place, he argues that in 1 Timothy 2, where Paul states a woman can have no authority over men, that the original text was not written by Paul but by a next-generation church leader.[57] He footnotes a reference to one of his other books to validate the point, yet builds his argument here on a very debatable premise.

The *Dallas Morning News* picks up on another of Ehrman's controversies regarding women in the New Testament:

> Another passage, instructing women to keep quiet in church, is found in First Corinthians. While scholars generally accept that Paul wrote that epistle, some early manuscripts place that passage in different places - evidence, Dr. Ehrman said, that it may have been added by a later scribe.[58]

1 Corinthians 14 falls as another of the controversial passages addressed in this section. He contends that the text is unoriginal, added by a later scribe. In his words, "The passage appears to be a clear and straightforward injunction for women not to speak (let alone teach!) in the church…"[59]

---

[54] http://www.boston.com/ae/books/articles/2006/04/12/the_new_profits_of_christianity/

[55] *Misquoting Jesus*, p. 179.

[56] *Ibid*, p. 180.

[57] *Ibid*, p. 182.

[58] http://www.dallasnews.com/sharedcontent/dws/news/localnews/stories/DN-biblesays_16rel.ART.State.Edition2.3e66907.html

[59] *Misquoting Jesus*, p. 183.

However, the evidence seems to not be clearly presented for the original text.[60] Bock notes:

> Ehrman fails to point out that: (1) most manuscripts, including the earliest ones, have the "keep silent" verse at the point of v. 34, and (2) no known manuscript that has this entire passage lacks the "keep silent" verse in chapter 14.[61]

Dr. Craig Blomberg of Denver Seminary agrees. In his review on *Misquoting Jesus*, he specifically points out the fallacy with this particular passage:

> Few textual critics of any theological stripe (including Fee) elsewhere accept as probable suggestions that the originals of any New Testament book read differently from all known copies, because of the sheer number and antiquity of the copies that we have, until a passage becomes too awkward for their overall theological systems (and even then most seek some other resolution of the tension than textual emendation).[62]

While the textual issues on verses 34-35 may be beyond the scope of this book, Blomberg's comments highlight the most important issue. Furthermore, as the NET Bible's notes on these verses state, there is not a single manuscript of 1 Corinthians 14 that does not include these verses. The issue is rather in their placement within the chapter.[63]

Another problematic passage is found in Acts 17:4. Here, he notes that our modern translations state: "And some of them were persuaded and joined with Paul and Silas, as did a great many of the pious Greeks, along with a large number of prominent women." He rightly notes that some manuscripts instead change the ending of the verse to read, "…along with a large number of wives of prominent men." The change makes the men prominent, leaving the wives out of the picture. Certainly, the manuscript evidence does support Ehrman's claim. There are some manuscripts that reword this portion. However, he fails to point out that no modern translation takes this view. Why? Because this is the minority view in the manuscript tradition. Once again, Ehrman cites an extreme and presents it as the norm.

---

60 Manuscripts D, F, G, and a few manuscripts from the Latin version have the "keep silent" verses after what is now v. 40: "all things should be done decently and In order." http://www.beliefnet.com/story/188/story_18803_1.html
[61]http://www.beliefnet.com/story/188/story_18803_1.html
[62] http://www.denverseminary.edu/dj/articles2006/0200/0206.php
[63] http://www.bible.org/netbible/index.htm, notes on 1 Corinthians 14:34-35.

He does the same with the use of the names of Aquila and Priscilla throughout Acts and in Romans 16:3. His argument is that scribes placed the female name second even though this was not the original reading. While this is true in some manuscripts, the motivations may not always be as controversial as Ehrman presses. For instance, even today in American culture, it is more common to introduce a married couple as "Mr. and Mrs. Johnson" rather than "Mrs. and Mr. Johnson." Neither option is necessarily right or wrong. It is simply a cultural norm of the English language.

The same would have been true of scribes in the early church. Luke (in Acts) and Paul (in Romans) may have specifically placed Priscilla first in places, but later scribes could have changed the word order due to a variety of reasons. 1) The change may have been due to thinking that the original must have placed the man first, 2) the change may have been an unintentional change, since the cultural mindset would have been to place the man first, 3) the copy the scribe copied from may have actually already been changed previously by another scribe, or 4) the scribe intentionally changed the word order, as Ehrman argues, due to views regarding women in the church.

Of at least four options on this issue, Ehrman's argument only includes one viewpoint. In doing so, his readers can easily be mislead to think there is no other option. Certainly this is not the case. While I agree that some manuscripts make the changes in word order he suggests, it is in no way certain that the scribes were pushing an anti-feminist church agenda.

The summary of this section in *Misquoting Jesus* states, "In short, there were debates in the early centuries of the church over the role of women, and on occasion these debates spilled over into the textual transmission of the New Testament itself, as scribes sometimes changed their texts in order to make them coincide more closely with the scribes' own sense of the (limited) role of women in the church."[64]

However, his conclusion appears only partially correct. Yes, debates about women in the early church certainly existed. Yes, in a few manuscripts there are changes that *could* be considered an influence of male superiority. However, to say this problem existed to the level Ehrman mentions is a far overstatement. In each case, an original text can be determined based on the overwhelming level of manuscript evidence for a particular reading.

After identifying and discussing each of the verses Ehrman presents in this section regarding women, Bock accurately states, "When we consider all of the

---

[64] *Misquoting Jesus*, p. 186.

evidence, we can eliminate the impression of damaging or intentional distortion."[65]

---

[65] http://www.beliefnet.com/story/188/story_18803_1.html

Chapter 10: How Can Evangelicals Respond to *Misquoting Jesus*?

Evangelical Christians have often compounded controversies regarding God's Word due to overreacting or under-reacting. Take, for instance, the recent phenomenon of *The Da Vinci Code*. Over twenty-seven books were written in response from a Christian orientation (as many as the number of New Testament books!), hitting every angle conceivable.[66]

Unfortunately, many of the attacks were not necessarily a "What would Jesus do?" approach. Not only were the titles sometimes unnecessarily critical (Remember *The Da Vinci Deception*?), but many of the sermons and books were completely hateful toward the author Dan Brown, film producer Ron Howard, actor Tom Hanks, and other involved in the film's making. While much good came from the writings of gracious and well-meaning individuals (Darrell Bock, John Ankerberg, Michael Easley, James Garlow, Erwin Lutzer, and Josh McDowell to name a few), the Church has hopefully learned a few more lessons that can be of help in responding to non-fiction works such as *Misquoting Jesus* that can help us in defending our faith, but also speaking the truth in love as the Apostle Paul taught.

Remember when *The Da Vinci Code* film released? Christians responded with one of several options:

1. Boycott It

Unfortunately, boycotting a book that has already sold 60 million copies doesn't hurt anyone's pocketbook. While it makes sense not to endorse a film that speaks poorly of Christ, running away communicated that Christians not only despised the film, but that they were scared of it. For some reason, even very educated individuals fought a valiant though losing effort to boycott the film. Among the most popular was the petition launched by Dr. Ted Baehr, founder and publisher of Movieguide.org and chairman of the Christian Film & Television Commission. As the film approached, he sent the following letter to thousands of Americans:

---

[66] I admit that I was part of this group, coauthoring *The Da Vinci Code Controversy* (Moody Publishing) as well as the Amazon Shorts title *The Use of the Bible in The Da Vinci Code*.

```
WE CHOOSE NOT TO SUPPORT BLASPHEMY

    An open letter to Christians and people of good will
about the upcoming film, The Da Vinci Code

    We the undersigned are on record that we will not buy
movie tickets for the film, The Da Vinci Code. The director
Ron Howard has promised he is being faithful to the
bestselling novel as he adapts it to the big screen. That
means the movie will likely be blasphemous, just as the book
is.

    The book is a novel but in telling its story, it makes
massive claims about Jesus Christ -- that He was not divine,
that He was secretly married, and that the "New Testament is
false propaganda." We recognize that while the movie may
give Christians a good opportunity to talk about faith
issues, millions of people -- not familiar in the least with
the Gospels -- could be spiritually poisoned with "false
propaganda" against Christ. This is especially true of
children.

    Since every movie ticket purchased is a VOTE, saying,
"Yes, Hollywood, make more movies like this!," we choose not
to buy a ticket for this movie. We choose not to support the
blasphemy. While recognizing this is an issue of conscience
and that people of good will may differ on how to approach
the film, this is how we choose to act. And we ask
Christians and all people of good will to consider doing
likewise.

    P.S. -- If you need more information to be familiar with
the story to intelligently discuss it with your parishioners
or acquaintances, please seek out good information. These
sites will help you: www.thetruthaboutdavinci.com and
www.davinciantidote.com. Or get the Da Vinci Code White
Paper at www.movieguide.org.⁶⁷
```

Did it work? Hardly! Unfortunately, Dr. Baehr's tactic only further alienated him from the general public, providing a negative example many others have fought to overcome.

2. "Other-cott" It

Some Christians (thousands!) actually believed that instead of boycotting the film, they could cast their vote by watching a *different* movie that was more

---

[67] http://www.humaneventsonline.com/article.php?id=14572.

family-friendly. The most common film was *Over the Hedge* by DreamWorks. Barbara Nicolosi is the founder and director of Act One (http://www.actoneprogram.com), an organization whose mission is to train committed Christian writers to work in the Hollywood film industry. At the *Christianity Today* website (Evangelical Christianity's most popular news magazine), she posted the "other-cott" view, saying:

> Let's rock the box office in a way no one expects—
> without protests, without boycotts, without arguments,
> without rancor. Let's show up at the box office ballot box
> and cast our votes. And buy some popcorn, too.
>
> As for The Da Vinci Code, don't go see this stupid
> movie. Don't pay money to have the insidious lies of the
> enemy introduced into your heart and mind.
>
> Let's "othercott" DVC on May 19 by going to see Over the
> Hedge instead.[68]

The numbers, however, showed the flaw in this reaction. *Da Vinci Code*, $77 million. *Over the Hedge*, $12 million opening weekend. Worldwide, the *Da Vinci Code* film marked the second highest opening weekend ever, with over $224 million in sales. Clearly, this approach did not achieve its desired impact.

3. Dialogue with It

I admit that I was one of the millions watching *The Da Vinci Code* film opening weekend. In fact, I took my pastor and an elder (and our wives!). Yet that Sunday we were able to discuss the film intelligently, share the truth and fiction, and help people learn how to handle the issue with their friends and coworkers.

Applying What We've Learned

In the case of *Misquoting Jesus*, I have again chosen to dialogue with it. The truth of the Bible can withstand any attack, and this case is no exception. In addressing some of the critical controversies at stake, my hope is to help readers like you better understand the important issues from a biblical perspective.

68

http://www.christianitytoday.com/channels/movies/commentaries/othercott.html

So, how *should* you respond to *Misquoting Jesus*? Let me offer the following positive options:

1. Don't Fear the Controversy

As you have seen throughout *Misquotes in Misquoting Jesus*, the facts show there are significant weaknesses at certain points in *Misquoting Jesus*. Though you may not have every answer for one of the world's top scholars on New Testament texts and early Christianity, you should certainly not fear that the Bible's accuracy or inspiration is undermined because of this book's views.

2. Seek the Truth

While "Seek the Truth" served as a tagline for *The Da Vinci Code*'s movie ads, it also serves as a fitting response to differing opinions on the Bible's integrity. In order to properly discuss issues like the transmission of the Bible, it is important to study what you *do* believe. This includes:

- Personal Bible reading (first and foremost)
- Reading about Church History
- Studying basic textual criticism
- Listening to radio broadcasts, podcasts, or CD programs on biblical issues
- Attending church services, seminars, and other educational opportunities

The more you understand what you *do* believe, the more comfortably you can handle arguments you do *not* believe.

3. Dialogue with Grace

Some people tend to switch into "attack mode" when someone confronts their belief system with a differing view. Unfortunately, this rarely helps the situation. Even in the case of this book, I have sought to politely share what I understand are accurate differences with Dr. Ehrman's book.

In fact, Appendix 2 of this book shows the actual emails Dr. Ehrman and I shared back and forth during the making of this book. Granted, I did not tell him the book's title, but was very clear that I wanted to offer him an opportunity to offer his thoughts on *Misquoting Jesus* from his own perspective. Anyone reading the conversation would agree I showed no personal antagonism. The goal was always to understand his view, rather than attacking him as a person.

The same principle applies from a reading of his book as well. Instead of declaring Ehrman some demonic monster set to destroy the church, seek to understand his viewpoint, pray for him as a person, and respectful share and live out your convictions. In doing so, perhaps positive change will occur that would live out the example of Christ from the New Testament in the eyes of someone who has seen much of the negative side of Christianity.

A Final Word

```
     "Every central doctrine of the faith is well-
established," he said. "Even if you take out all the
readings he [Dr. Ehrman] has suggested in his book, you have
not altered Christianity as a whole."⁶⁹
```

This quick look regarding the controversies in *Misquoting Jesus* has been provided as a tool to assist you in better understanding your faith and communicating it with others. As you discuss *Misquoting Jesus* at the office, school, gym, boardroom, or local coffee shop, remember Paul's instruction to speak the truth in love (Ephesians 4:15). Do not fear speaking out about what you believe. This is God's desire for us. Yet he also values our love for every person we encounter, whether they wholeheartedly agree with our values or mock at our so-called "simple-minded" beliefs.

Ultimately, Jesus gave up his rights for the cross to show the power of his great love for all humanity. As you walk out your faith, show grace, act in love, and speak with knowledge regarding the things God's Word says are true. I pray God greatly uses you to help shape hearts and minds for Christ. May God bless you in your efforts to share the words of truth!

---

⁶⁹http://www.dallasnews.com/sharedcontent/dws/news/localnews/stories/DN-biblesays_16rel.ART.State.Edition2.3e66907.html by Darrell Bock.

Appendix A: What People Are Saying About *Misquoting Jesus*

From blogs to book reviews, people of every kind have begun sounding off regarding their likes and dislikes on *Misquoting Jesus*. The following list includes a few of the interesting quotes and comments I discovered while researching this topic. Please note that I do not necessarily agree or endorse any of these views. They are simply included for your greater understanding of how others have commented on the issue.

> "The book's very title is a bit too provocative and misleading though: Almost none of the variants that Ehrman discusses involve *sayings* by Jesus! The book simply doesn't deliver what the title promises."
>
> -Dr. Dan Wallace at http://www.bible.org/page.asp?page_id=3452

✝ ✝ ✝

> "Ehrman, as noted, has a tendency to simply create problems where none exist, and then expects readers to share his overzealous worry. Semantics dictates that his concern to have the "very words" [5] of the original, inspired text is misplaced. Communication is simply not that difficult to achieve. Nor does it stand well as a claim made in a book where he claims to be solving and explaining the very things he says are problems."
>
> -J.P. Holding in a review at http://www.tektonics.org/books/ehrqurvw.html.

✝ ✝ ✝

> "Thus his first extended examples of textual problems in the New Testament are the woman caught in adultery and the longer ending of Mark. After demonstrating how neither of these is likely to be part of the originals of either Gospel, Ehrman concedes that 'most of the changes are not of this magnitude' (p. 69). But this sounds as if there are at least a few others that are of similar size, when in fact there are no other textual variants anywhere that are even one-fourth as long as these thirteen- and twelve-verse additions…

One surprising factual error occurs when Ehrman insists that Acts 4:13 means that Peter and John were illiterate (the term agrammatos—'unlettered' in this context means not educated beyond the elementary education accessible to most first-century Jewish boys)."

- Craig L. Blomberg, Distinguished Professor of New Testament, Denver Seminary, February 2006, at http://www.denverseminary.edu/dj/articles2006/0200/0206.php.

✝✝✝

"Ehrman's second overall argument (spread through a number of chapters) is that the manuscripts themselves are so chocked full of scribal mistakes and inconsistencies that they cannot be trusted. The reader senses Ehrman's excitement about being able to cite such large numbers of textual variants and it seems that he is expecting that his readers will be stunned by these figures ("some say there are 200,000 variants known, some say 300,000, some say 400,000 or more!", p.89). He even appeals to John Mill's 1707 edition of the Greek New Testament (more particularly, its critical apparatus) in which Mill catalogued thirty thousand textual differences with the various manuscripts in his possession. Ehrman proceeds to further emphasize the "problem" of textual variations by providing a brief history of textual criticism in chapter four, highlighting how various scholars struggled over the years to find a way to recover the original text of the New Testament. Again, several comments are in order. (a) Ehrman's use of numbers here is a bit misleading because he never makes it clear to the reader that the vast, vast, majority of these textual differences are typical, run-of-the-mill, scribal variations that do not affect the integrity of the text in the least (misspellings, word order changes, omitted words, etc.) Indeed, once a person realizes that such changes are a normal part of the transmission of any historical document, then they cease to be relevant for the discussion of the New Testament's reliability (lest all antiquity slip into obscurity). Such variants should be expected in historical documents, not put forth as scandalous. But, this is precisely the point Ehrman refuses to make clear to the reader. (b) Ehrman's numerical barrage also does not take into account the vast number of manuscripts we possess. Obviously, if we only possessed say, five manuscripts of the New Testament, then we would have very few textual variants to account for. But, we have over 5000 Greek manuscripts alone (not to mention the various versions), more than any other document of antiquity. Thus, a pure numerical count of variants is misleading: of course they will increase because the number of manuscripts is vastly increased. In many ways, therefore, Christianity is a victim of its own success. While the vast number of manuscripts should be positive historical evidence and indicative of the New Testament's

authenticity, Ehrman, somehow, turns the tables to make it
evidence for its tendentious character—a remarkable feat to
be sure. Unfortunately, the person left in the dark here is
the average reader. On p.87 Ehrman even acknowledges this
point (originally made by Bentley years ago), but never
offers a response to it. (c) In addition to these
considerations, Ehrman also does not mention that the vast
majority of these textual variants are easily spotted and
easily corrected. Indeed, the entire science of textual
criticism (of which Ehrman is an obvious proponent) is
committed to this very task. But, Ehrman almost gives the
impression that 400,000 variants exist and we have no idea
what was original and what was not, throwing the entire New
Testament into utter obscurity. That is simply misleading."

Michael Kruger, Associate Professor of New Testament at
Reformed Theological Seminary in Charlotte, NC
http://reformation21.com/Shelf_Life/Shelf_Life/181/?vobId=29
30&pm=434

✞ ✞ ✞

Finally, the book is filled with statements presented as
fact that are, in reality, hotly disputed. Ehrman believes,
for example, in the existence of the document known as "Q"
and that Luke and Matthew both copied liberally from the
book of Mark. He believes that the book of 1 Timothy was not
written by Paul and that several important passages
throughout the gospels and epistles were not original but
appended to the documents at a later date by people with a
specific agenda. If the reader does not agree with these
presuppositions, much of the book's argument dissolves.

http://www.dietofbookworms.com/title.php?id=594

✞ ✞ ✞

A prolific writer, Ehrman has become a relentless
skeptic of the traditional understanding of the New
Testament, its message, and its history. He has appeared on
CNN, the Discovery Channel, and even Jon Stewart's *Daily
Show*. And he delights in "taking something really
complicated and getting a sound bite out of it."

Gary Burge, "The Lapsed Evangelic Critic" in
Christianity Today, June 2006, pg. 24. Accessed online at
www.christianitytoday.com/ct/2006/006/11.26.html.

Appendix B: An E-Conversation with Bart Ehrman

```
From: Dillon Burroughs [mailto:dillonburroughs@hotmail.com]
Sent: Wednesday, May 24, 2006 12:34 PM
To: Bart Ehrman
Subject: Your thoughts
```

Dr. Ehrman,

I am currently working on a book that provides an evangelical response on your views presented in your bestselling book Misquoting Jesus. While my views represent a contrast with those in your work, I would greatly appreciate any personal thoughts you may want to share in preparation for its release this Fall.

Specifically, I would request about 15 minutes via phone where I could ask specific questions regarding behind the scene information on the making of Misquoting Jesus. If this would be declined, I would at least like to send a handful of questions via email for your response.

Please know that my intentions in this research will not be a radical personal attack or anything of the like. I am specifically looking at the book's materials and challenging specific arguments in order to provide a conservative evangelical perspective for readers of your book asking how others would handle these issues.

I look forward to hearing from you soon. My personal cell number is ##### if you need it.

Sincerely,

Dillon Burroughs

✝ ✝ ✝

NIMBLE BOOKS LLC

From: Bart Ehrman 12:03 PM 5/24/06
To: "'Dillon Burroughs'" <dillonburroughs@hotmail.com>
Subject: RE: Your thoughts

Dillon,

May I ask what exactly you're refuting? Surely not that there are
variations in the manuscripts in the New Testament and that there
are large debates over what the text says in places! Do you have
any training in this field?

-- BDE

Bart D. Ehrman
James A. Gray Professor
Department of Religious Studies
University of North Carolina at Chapel Hill

✞ ✞ ✞

From: Dillon Burroughs [mailto:dillonburroughs@hotmail.com]
Sent: Wednesday, May 24, 2006 3:33 PM
To: Bart Ehrman
Subject: RE: Your thoughts

Dr. Ehrman,

Thanks for your prompt response. My goal is to present an
evangelical response to those views which differ from the "norm"
in conservative churches. I certainly agree with the fact that
there are variations in N.T. manuscripts. It's rather the
conclusions one makes based on those differences that concerns me.
My contention is that the differences do not necessarily mean a
person cannot hold to inerrancy. This is not just a belief based
on deductive analysis but a deeply held theological belief agreed
upon by people of faith based on the concept that the text
represents God's Word and is "God-breathed."

In terms of personal training, I do hold a ThM from an evangelical
seminary and have studied Greek for three years at the graduate
level, including one semester of study with Dr. Dan Wallace, a
name I think you would recognize. I don't claim to be a textual
criticism expert, but at least understand the issues involved.

I understand if you have no interest in communicating further.
However, I do want to extend an opportunity to share your thoughts
as you wish. Thanks again for your time.

Sincerely,

Dillon

✝ ✝ ✝

From: Bart Ehrman 2:41 PM 5/24/06
To: "'Dillon Burroughs'" <dillonburroughs@hotmail.com>
Subject: RE: Your thoughts

That's interesting; so you think that the originals were inerrant,
but that we don't have the originals?

Bart D. Ehrman
James A. Gray Professor
Department of Religious Studies
University of North Carolina at Chapel Hill

✝ ✝ ✝

From: Dillon Burroughs (dillonburroughs@hotmail.com) 4:28 PM
5/24/06
To: "Bart Ehrman"
Subject: RE: Your thoughts

Thanks again for your reply. Since you seem to be at least open to
discussion, here are my main questions regarding *Misquoting Jesus*:

1. How did the project come about?
2. What are your thoughts on the strong response to the book's
sales?
3. How did some of your major media exposure come about on this
project? For instance, not many professors get invited to the
Daily Show, but you seemed to be a hit. What was that like?
4. How do you feel about some of the critics who have responded
strongly against your arguments in Misquoting Jesus?
5. What future projects or writings are out there next that we
should be watching out for?

And, to answer your question, I believe that though we do not have
the original NT manuscripts, we can determine with great accuracy
what the original was in most cases and that those points that are
questionable do not have to be as shaking to a person's faith as
they have been for some who have rejected the idea of an inspired
NT because we cannot have an exact 100 percent accuracy. Long
sentence, I know, but that's my take on it. Thanks!

Dillon

[Note: As of this point, this is the end of the e-conversation. No further responses
were received.]

Appendix C: Resources for Learning About Textual Criticism

While New Testament Textual Criticism remains a somewhat obscure field of study, several resources now exist that make the information more accessible to the everyday reader. I've included what I consider some of the best books and websites on this issue for those interested in a "do it yourself" approach in evaluating the claims of *Misquoting Jesus*.

Books:

Aland, K. and B. *The Text of the New Testament*. G.R.: Eerdmans, 1989.

Black, D.A. *New Testament Textual Criticism: A Concise Guide*. G.R.: Baker, 1994.

Greenlee, J. H. *Introduction to New Testament Textual Criticism*. Peabody: Hendrickson, 1995.

Metzger, B. M. *A Textual Commentary on the Greek New Testament*. London & N.Y.: United Bible Societies, 1994.

A special thanks to the research provided by Denver Seminary at http://www.denverseminary.edu/dj/articles2005/0200/0201.php for the above resource listing.

For a complete list of textual criticism books from a Christian perspective, go to www.christianbook.com and search by keyword using "textual criticism." There you will find 68 books, including some of the titles listed above.

Websites:

Interpreting Ancient Manuscripts Web
http://www.earlham.edu/~seidti/iam/interp_mss.html

By Timothy Seid: well designed, user friendly introduction to new Testament Textual Criticism featuring short essays, images, an exercise and a manuscript catalogue.

The Encyclopedia of New Testament Textual Criticism

http://www.skypoint.com/~waltzmn/

Conceived by Rich Elliott and created by Robert B. Waltz: lots of articles arranged in an easily accessible index format, regularly updated.

New Testament Papyri and Codices

http://www.kchanson.com/papyri.html

By K. C. Hanson: a useful, well laid-out catalogue featuring introductory bibliography.

Complete List of Greek NT Papyri

http://www-user.uni-bremen.de/~wie/texte/Papyri-list.html

By Wieland Willker: another useful catalogue, limited to Greek NT Papyri.

TC Links

http://rosetta.reltech.org/TC/TC-links.html

The links section of Textual Criticism, maintained by Jimmy Adair, provides a comprehensive guide to material on the internet material on Biblical textual criticism.

A Synoptic Gospels Primer

http://virtualreligion.net/primer/gloss.html

By Mahlon Smith: useful introductions to Codex Bezae, Codex, Diatessaron, Manuscript, Minuscule, Oxyrhynchus, Papyrus, Parchment, P^{64} & P^{67}, Recension, Sinaiticus, Textual Criticism, Textus Receptus, Uncial, Vaticanus and Vellum.

Student's Guide to New Testament Textual Variants

http://bible.ovc.edu/tc/index.htm

By Bruce Terry: some fine introductory material for students, with a breakdown of each NT book into sections. Greek not required.

The Oldest Extant Editions of the Letters of Paul

http://www.religion-online.org/showarticle.asp?title=91

By David Trobisch: a new, illustrated on-line article by Prof. David Trobisch of Bangor Theological Seminary, U.S.A., adapted from the first chapter of the author's *Paul's Letter Collection: Tracing the Origins* (Fortress Press: Minneapolis, 1994).

Codex Vaticanus

http://www-user.uni-bremen.de/~wie/Vaticanus/index.html By Wieland Willker: clear, illustrated web site devoted to Codex Vaticanus (B/03), including reflections on the recently discovered text-critical "umlaut" signs. This is a valuable addition to the extensive materials already made available on Wieland Willker's Bible Pages.

A special thanks to Dr Mark Goodacre from the Department of Theology at the University of Birmingham and his website at www.ntgateway.com for these listed websites.

Appendix D: Additional Books by Bart Ehrman

The following list includes published books in print by Dr. Bart Ehrman. For a complete bibliography of additional written materials, articles, and edited works, please see http://www.unc.edu/depts/rel_stud/faculty/BartDEhrman/BartCV.htm.

Ehrman, Bart (2006). *Peter, Paul, and Mary Magdalene: The Followers of Jesus in History and Legend*, Oxford University Press, USA. ISBN 0195300130.

Ehrman, Bart (2005). *Misquoting Jesus: The Story Behind Who Changed the Bible and Why*, HarperSanFrancisco. ISBN 0060738170.

Metzger, Bruce M.; Ehrman, Bart (2005). *The Text of the New Testament: Its Transmission, Corruption, and Restoration*, Oxford University Press, USA. ISBN 0195166671.

Ehrman, Bart (2004). *Truth and Fiction in The Da Vinci Code: A Historian Reveals What We Really Know about Jesus, Mary Magdalene, and Constantine*, Oxford University Press, USA. ISBN 0195181409.

Ehrman, Bart (2004). *A Brief Introduction to the New Testament*, Oxford University Press, USA. ISBN 0195161238.

Ehrman, Bart (2003). *The Lost Christianities: The Battles for Scripture and the Faiths We Never Knew*, Oxford University Press, USA. ISBN 0195141830.

Ehrman, Bart (2003). *The New Testament: A Historical Introduction to the Early Christian Writings*, Oxford University Press, USA. ISBN 0195154622.

Ehrman, Bart; Jacobs, Andrew S. (2003). *Christianity in Late Antiquity, 300-450 C.E.: A Reader*, Oxford University Press, USA. ISBN 0195154614.

Ehrman, Bart (2003). *The Apostolic Fathers: Volume II. Epistle of Barnabas. Papias and Quadratus. Epistle to Diognetus. The Shepherd of Hermas*, Harvard University Press. ISBN 0674996089.

Ehrman, Bart (2003). *The Apostolic Fathers: Volume I. I Clement. II Clement. Ignatius. Polycarp. Didache,* Harvard University Press. ISBN 0674996070.

Ehrman, Bart (2003). *The New Testament and Other Early Christian Writings: A Reader,* Oxford University Press, USA. ISBN 0195154649.

Ehrman, Bart (2003). *Lost Scriptures: Books that Did Not Make It into the New Testament,* Oxford University Press, USA. ISBN 0195141822.

Ehrman, Bart (1999). *Jesus: Apocalyptic Prophet of the New Millennium,* Oxford University Press, USA. ISBN 019512474X.

Ehrman, Bart (1998). *After the New Testament: A Reader in Early Christianity,* Oxford University Press, USA. ISBN 0195114450.

Ehrman, Bart (1996). *The Orthodox Corruption of Scripture: The Effect of Early Christological Controversies on the Text of the New Testament,* Oxford University Press, USA. ISBN 0195102797.

Ehrman, Bart (1987). *Didymus the Blind and the Text of the Gospels (The New Testament in the Greek Fathers; No. 1),* Society of Biblical Literature. ISBN 1555400841.

Courtesy of Wikipedia at http://en.wikipedia.org/wiki/Bart_D._Ehrman.

Appendix E:
Information Launch Pad

W. Frederick Zimmerman

This appendix provides a concise survey of selected Internet information resources on the Internet that can help you learn more about *Misquoting Jesus.*

Amazon.com Information

We'll start with Amazon.com, which is much more than just a place to buy the book.

SALES RANKS

The reason we're all here is that *Misquoting Jesus* has been a best-seller. If you want to gauge whether people in your congregation are talking about *Misquoting Jesus,* the current Amazon.com sales rank is a pretty good place to start.

Misquoting Jesus has been among the best-selling religious books on Amazon[70] since it was published.

Services like Titlez.com[71] provide an interesting historical view of the sales popularity of *Misquoting Jesus.*

Figure E-1. Titlez.com sales ranks for *Misquoting Jesus,* Nov. 2005 – June 2006

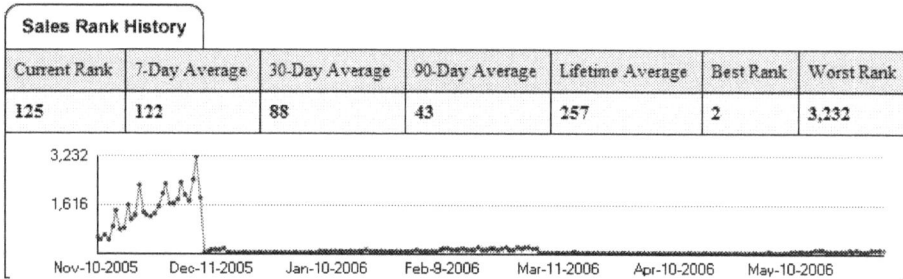

Current Rank	7-Day Average	30-Day Average	90-Day Average	Lifetime Average	Best Rank	Worst Rank
125	122	88	43	257	2	3,232

---

[70] http://www.amazon.com/exec/obidos/tg/new-for-you/top-sellers/-/books/22
[71] http://www.titlez.com

Direct page link: http://www.titlez.com/app/oneSheet.aspx?ASIN=0060738170

INSIDE THIS BOOK

If you're on a straight path to buy the book when you're at Amazon, you may skip over the "Inside the Book." That may be a mistake, as there is some very interesting stuff. For example, the Statistically Improbable Phrases feature, despite its forbiddingly technical name, offers a unique way of "getting the gist" of the book.   The statistically improbable phrases for *Misquoting Jesus* are:

- very human book,
- pagan opponents,
- inerrant word

Now the first and the last phrases make intuitive sense, but what are we to make of the middle one: "pagan opponents"? Apparently this is a phrase that Ehrman uses a lot that isn't very common in other books in the Amazon system. In fact, we discover, he is the leading user of this phrase. Amazon finds:

- 5 references in *Misquoting Jesus* : The Story Behind Who Changed the Bible and Why by Bart D. Ehrman

- 2 references in The Egyptian Hermes: A Historical Approach to the Late Pagan Mind by Garth Fowden

- 2 references in Lord Jesus Christ: Devotion to Jesus in Earliest Christianity by Larry W. Hurtado

- 1 reference in Capturing the Pagan Mind: Paul's Blueprint for Thinking and Living in the New Global Culture by Peter Jones

- 1 reference in The True Believer : Thoughts on the Nature of Mass Movements (Perennial Classics) by Eric Hoffer

- 1 reference in The Resurrection of the Son of God (Christian Origins and the Question of God) by N. T. Wright

- 1 reference in The Faith of the Early Fathers, Vol. 2 by William A. Jurgens

- 1 reference in <u>The Historical Jesus : The Life of a Mediterranean Jewish Peasant</u> by John Dominic Crossan

- 1 reference in <u>Islam for Dummies</u> by Malcolm Clark

- 1 reference in <u>In Search of Paul : How Jesus' Apostle Opposed Rome's Empire with God's Kingdom</u> by John Dominic Crossan, Jonathan L. Reed

- 1 reference in <u>Missiology: An Introduction to the Foundations, History, and Strategies of World Missions</u> by John Mark Terry (Editor), et al 1 reference in <u>Philippians (IVP New Testament Commentary Series)</u> by Gordon D. Fee, et al

- 1 reference in <u>Freemasonry and Its Ancient Mystic Rites</u> by C.W. Leadbeater

- 1 reference in <u>Gravity's Arc : The Story of Gravity from Aristotle to Einstein and Beyond</u> by David Darling

- 1 reference in <u>Witchcraft in Europe, 400-1700: A Documentary History (Middle Ages Series)</u> by Alan Charles Kors (Editor), Edward Peters (Editor)

- 1 reference in <u>One Hundred Saints: Their Lives and Likenesses Drawn from Butler's "Lives of the Saints" and Great Works of Western Art</u> by Bulfinch Press

- 1 reference in <u>Heroes Of The City Of Man</u> by Peter J. Leithart

- 1 reference in <u>After the New Testament : A Reader in Early Christianity</u> by Bart D. Ehrman (Editor)

- 1 reference in <u>The First Urban Christians: The Social World of the Apostle Paul</u> by Wayne A. Meeks

- 1 reference in <u>Revelation 1-7: An Exegetical Commentary (Wycliffe Exegetical Commentary)</u> by Robert L. Thomas

- 1 reference in <u>Learning Theology With the Church Fathers</u> by Christopher A. Hall.

In short, the SIP feature appears to show us, using reasonably objective data, that Bart Ehrman is a leading proponent of the concept that the Bible was developed in an oppositional process with pagan contemporaries. The concept apparently is adopted by a number of other authors, but no one else has made it the centerpiece of a book.

CONCORDANCE

The Inside the Book Concordance provides another intuitive way of "gisting" *Misquoting Jesus.*

Figure 2. Amazon.com Concordance for *Misquoting Jesus*

account among another appears author bible book called came century changed changes christ christian church come communities copied copies day death different does early edition end even example fact faith father first form found god gospel greek himself however human jesus jewish jews john kind know later letter luke man manuscripts mark may mean might new now number original others own part passage paul people places point problem read reading say scholars scribes scripture second see seen simply since sometimes son story testament text textual things though time tradition two variant verses view women words work world writings written years

If you're really in a pinch to explain *Misquoting Jesus,* just mumble "Jesus, manuscripts, scribes, text!"

Google

Google offers some useful tools for keeping track of news references and blogs pertaining to *Misquoting Jesus*.

GOOGLE NEWS

I have set up <u>a Google News search that alerts me every time there is a news story referring to *Misquoting Jesus*:</u>

<u>http://news.google.com/news?hl=en&ned=&q=misquoting+jesus&btnG=Search+ News</u>

I can receive the results either by e-mail as a Google Alert or as <u>RSS</u> in a news feed reader.[72]

GOOGLE BLOG SEARCH

Google Blog Search also provides a useful tool for <u>finding recent blog references to *Misquoting Jesus*.</u>

<u>http://blogsearch.google.com/blogsearch?hl=en&q=misquoting+jesus&btnG=Sear ch+Blogs</u>

---

[72] <u>http://news.google.com/news?hl=en&ned=&q=misquoting+jesus&ie=UTF-8&output=rss&ned=:ePkh8BM9VVBNa0JBDPTSPyCIx6Z7XARb8ODVj0OhFTw Ues5boy_0JSm7q- WBP97tWyr0FGbITCYzHm4s_cLpOXSEERqTxsEV7sQP4bfpP- pAFw7knh9quqmfuCOnxKbYdMW47MrZtCZ- 8o93IQnFE2noIRUYWsiE4uo_M-- 3lKNxhj2nbJqKzY5RGF4JcwFv1hCsY4869NCOX_x8x6HlEyp8WnehyEq_svfO- gNsMMYCPkykh5XgF8Xa5KjWOAz5q-8GQBtO-g</u>

Other Blog Search Engines

Other blog search engines, such as Technorati.com and Ask.com, are worth checking out because they offer the ability to sort results by "authority" or "popularity."

TECHNORATI.COM

A Technorati search on the quoted phrase "misquoting jesus":

http://www.technorati.com/search/%22misquoting%20jesus%22

ASK.COM

An Ask.com search on the quoted phrase "misquoting jesus":

http://www.ask.com/blogsearch?q=%22misquoting+jesus%22&t=a&s=p&ql=&qsrc=2104&rpp=10

A Christian Perspective on Harry Potter

Also available from Nimble Books: *Unauthorized Harry Potter Book 7 News: Half-Blood Prince Analysis and Speculation* by W. Frederick Zimmerman. ISBN: 0976540606. Available from Amazon.com and other fine on-line booksellers, or by special order from your local bookstore.

http://www.amazon.com/exec/obidos/ASIN/0976540606/

… The Harry Potter phenomenon has sparked a great deal of controversy among Christians. Obviously, my own view is that the Potter books are good for children; but as a Christian, I feel a responsibility to acknowledge and address the issues before encouraging readers to plunge into this book …

Mimi Cummmins, HPBook6.com
Kudos to the author for [a] very well written book [and] using new technologies that [keep] readers up to date.

Dave Haber, Executive Editor, WizardNews.com
… very heavily documented ... making this book an important source of information you'll want to refer to over and over again.

Harry Potter Automatic News Aggregator, HPANA.com
HPANA recommended book! --

Greg S. Davidson, Amazon reviewer
This is a pathfinder for a fundamentally new kind of book ... the author's prose is both lively and concise . . .

This "nimble" guide to the work of best-selling author J. K. Rowling takes advantage of the unique capabilities of electronic publishing technology to provide the latest news about the author and her works, updated whenever there are significant developments. Unlike a conventional book, for which editions are printed in quantity every couple of years, this "living book" goes through frequent "mini-editions" and is printed fresh whenever customers place an order.

A Christian Perspective on Dan Brown

Also available from Nimble Books: *The Solomon Key and Beyond: Unauthorized Dan Brown Update* by W. Frederick Zimmerman. ISBN: 0975447998.

Available from <u>Amazon.com</u> and other fine on-line booksellers, or by special order from your local bookstore.

<u>http://www.amazon.com/gp/product/0975447998</u>

… As a Christian I feel responsible to comment on the theology of The Da Vinci Code. Fortunately, my position is quite simple.

If, as I do, you accept that the Four Gospels (Matthew, Mark, Luke, and John) are the authentic, divinely inspired Word of God, then The Da Vinci Code is simply fiction–clever, enjoyable, provocative fiction, but fiction nonetheless. The reason is that there are too many statements in those Gospels that are completely inconsistent with the provocative ideas in The Da Vinci Code.

If, like many, you are not sure whether the Four Gospels are the final Word, I urge you to read The Da Vinci Code with a discerning mind. Start with the Bible as we have it today. If the theories Dan Brown puts forward had been found persuasive in previous centuries, his book would not be in the "fiction" section of the bookstore, and there would be a billion Gnostic Bibles in print, instead of a billion Bibles that affirm the divinity of Christ.

If you are a skeptic or an agnostic, have fun reading this work of fiction … but ask yourself once or twice, in the small wee hours of the morning when your soul is quiet, why is this particular thriller such a best seller? Can you come up with a respectful explanation of why the story of Christ is still so important to so many people? …

A Christian Perspective on
American Theocracy

Coming in Fall 2006 from Nimble Books: *American Theocracy Unpacked: Arguments Disassembled, Implications Examined, and a Way Forward Suggested* by W. Frederick Zimmerman. ISBN: 0-9777424-9-0

Available from Amazon.com and other fine on-line booksellers, or by special order from your local bookstore.

http://www.amazon.com/gp/product/0977742490

… When I began reading *American Theocracy*, the best-seller by Kevin Phillips, I felt almost immediately that this was an excellent and thought-provoking book that was so wrong about so many fundamental issues that it demanded a strong, immediate, and highly focused response. This book, American *Theocracy Unpacked,* takes advantage of electronic publishing technology to provide that "nimble" response, less than three months after I started reading Phillips's book.

In *American Theocracy Unpacked*, I take a close, almost paragraph-by-paragraph look at Phillips's arguments. I am confident that the result is respectful but stimulating. I acknowledge and applaud his many important insights, but I also suggest a way forward that is less fearful of an "American theocracy," and, indeed, more hopeful for America and the world…

Colophon

This book was produced using Microsoft Word and Adobe Acrobat. The cover was produced using The Gimp 2.0.2 with Ghostscript. The cover font is Arial.

Heading fonts and the body text inside the book are in Palatino Linotype, chosen because it is a nimble-looking font. Quotations are in Courier New, which is especially suitable in this case because the Gospels are also known as The Good News!

The American Heritage® Dictionary of the English Language, Fourth Edition, copyright © 2000 by Houghton Mifflin Company defines col·o·phon as follows:

```
    An ancient Greek city of Asia Minor northwest of
Ephesus. It was famous for its cavalry.
```

Along the same lines, Webster's Revised Unabridged, copyright 1996, 1998, MICRA, Inc.:

```
    \Col"o*phon\ (k[o^]l"[-o]*f[o^]n), n. [L. colophon
finishing stroke, Gr. kolofw`n; cf. L. culmen top, collis
hill. Cf. Holm.] An inscription, monogram, or cipher,
containing the place and date of publication, printer's
name, etc., formerly placed on the last page of a book.
```

Thus the etymology is reminiscent of the finishing stroke of a cavalry charge—the mounted horseman swinging his sword to vanquish a cowering opponent! For a book of this nature, what better final stroke could there be than the last words of Jesus?

```
    "It is finished." (John 19:30)
```

www.ingramcontent.com/pod-product-compliance
Lightning Source LLC
Chambersburg PA
CBHW031005090426

42737CB00008B/692